SEX-RATED

The Truth, The Lies, and The Mishaps

Laila Benzel

Copyright and Credits © 2021 Laila Benzel
ISBN: 978-0-620-95005-3 (Print)
Illustrator: Motsanaphe Morare (MoMaLifeLiving.com)
Editor and Proof-reader: Soneni Sonia Dube
(sdube@thegoldengooseinstitute.com)

I would love to hear from you. Your questions, your
comments are welcome. Don't be a stranger. My contact
information is listed below, and I encourage you to
contact me. I am also available for speaking
engagements.

My email address is moonjanelaila@gmail.com

This book was published by
The Golden Goose Institute (Pty) Ltd

For further information email:
info@thegoldengooseinstitute.com

REVIEWS

"Finally - a book that does not presume to teach us how we should have sex and how to become sex prodigies, but one that offers a good opportunity to learn about the cultural relationships and perceptions of other people like us. Their experiences push us to confront and reflect on what sex is for ourselves."

Enrico Caporello,
—Doctor (Italy)

"The book scrutinizes the most crucial issues humans face with regards to sex and provides insight and deep knowledge around the subject. This is a perfect book for our time, and for both youngsters and adults: readers will definitely be captivated. It is doubtful many books have dealt as honestly and as enthusiastically with the complexity of sex as Laila Benzel has through this work."

Mulalo Madula,
—Speaker & Economist (South Africa)

"'God made sex and He made it good.' This is a statement that would shock most people but not Laila - her candid approach to the topic is refreshing and much needed in this generation. If you want a biblical understanding of sex and a view of how God really sees things, buy this book."

Pastor Marco Jacobs
—(South Africa)

DEDICATION

Dad, this is for you!
In loving memory of Manuel Jose Monjane

*Your life was snatched away from us during the
Covid-19 pandemic but the fond memories of you
– your love, strength, and wisdom - will live on in me
forever. Just as you have touched, impacted, and
changed many lives, I would hope that my footprints
will be drawn in people's hearts through my life and
this book.*

FOREWORD

I can remember overhearing my friends talk about sex. I was 16 at the time and still a virgin. I would hear how pleasing it was and my curiosity at the time had me thinking, "I wonder what sex feels like and when I will get my turn in experiencing this *'magic'* my friends are talking about?"

All I knew about sex at that point in time was what I had watched on T.V., seen in magazines filled with naked women, and viewed in pornographic videos. Although these images, whether still or moving, were stimulating, the mystery of what *sex really* felt like always had me intensely curious: "Would she moan? Would she tell me I was a man afterward? Would I have the stamina that would last all night long? Was I 'big' enough?" An interesting thing about questions, is eventually they get their answers.

Fast track to the age of 18, in one moment, I received my answers all in the affirmative.

While that moment resulted in a boost to my ego, there was a resounding emptiness that I felt after my encounter. As usual, I asked myself a couple of questions: "Why does sex feel great before and during the act, but afterward it leaves you with a large sense of emptiness?" These questions eventually found their answers too.

12 years on from the age of 18, when I began to practice celibacy, it dawned on me that I had been missing a connection. Before celibacy, whether I liked the person that I was dating or not, once sex was introduced, everything would begin to change. The relationship would begin to take a nose-dive and would eventually end. I would make sex important and made all the relationships I was in subservient to it. This made room for a lot of heartbreak which up till now, I am not pleased about.

As I read this book, which I completed in one sitting, it dawned on me that many others have been on the same journey and perhaps if they were as courageous as Laila to share and get conversations about sex started, it may have allowed someone like myself to have asked a different set of questions. Questions that I now know would have found their answers.

I would have asked, "Why do people have sex? Does it matter who they have sex with? When is it the right time to have sex? Is there a right time? Do I really want to have sex or is it just the material that I have encountered that has me curious?" The answers to these I know would have had me on a different trajectory.

Now I cannot change the past, nor do I choose to. I do, however, want to walk into a brighter future wiser than I was before.

And so, if you like me are asking the questions I had when I was a teenager, then this is the book for you. If you, like me are asking yourself the second batch of questions then this book is for you. Lastly, if you, like me are asking yourself the third batch of questions, then this book is for you. It will have you a lot wiser and a lot more equipped on all things pertaining to sex. A bonus is the experiences from other individuals who have chosen to also share their stories. It really allowed me to feel like I was not alone in asking the questions I had and that I was not an outlier either. Feelings I am certain to some extent you have felt.

As you become enlightened, which I know you will, I ask that you do two things:

1. Read the book from start to finish.
2. Start having the conversation of sex with those who are around you and with those you care for. You will be better for it.

Laila, thank you for putting this together, and although it has taken you 10 years to manifest, I know the words in this book will save people years of pain, and add multiple years of fulfilment."

Grant Senzani,
— Author, Publisher & Speaker (Malawi)

TABLE OF CONTENTS

HOW TO READ
THIS BOOK

L et's start with a little mental exercise. You have thoughts around the topic of sex - beliefs, scepticism, convictions, frustrations, experiences, things people told you, things you have read and opinions amongst other things. Imagine those thoughts as marbles, each one having a tint of shine.

Got it? Good! Now take those marbles and put them in a bucket, or a cup holder in your car, or even your pocket or old handbag. You get the point? Set them aside and put them out of sight just for a little while. But because this is a book of stories of real people who have experienced real things, whenever you feel like you relate and you need one or two of those marbles for personal reference, pick them up, peruse them, and feel them on the tips of your fingers for a while then set them aside again. If you do this you will not feel condemned or have any ideas that mis-construe your judgment.

It will simply be a book of heartfelt stories, research, and biblical analogies that are there for your enjoyment, and maybe, just maybe, may make you think or feel differently about your marbles.

Please note that you will find true stories of people that were interviewed by the author. These interviews include people from various countries including South Africa, Nigeria, the USA, Italy, and Germany to mention a few. All names have been changed to protect the identity of the individuals.

EXTRA CAUTION

As mentioned before, in this book we have a few biblical analogies and quotes, so here are a few thoughts before we get rolling:

Disclaimer

When determining what a verse really means, it is absolutely essential to look at the context, and to interpret individual verses in light of the Bible as a whole. "Proof texting," or using individual verses without considering context is dangerous. Anyone can quote scripture that would promote almost any viewpoint, even ones that run counter to what the text actually teaches So, how can you trust that I'm interpreting these verses correctly? Honestly, I recommend that you don't take my word for it. Check out the verses in context for yourself, using your own knowledge, understanding, and wisdom.

"Firstly, the bible is not a Christian book. I say that because many people have come to understand the bible as a book for a certain group of people to claim, own and then help them divide themselves from everyone else. But the bible is a book on what it means to be human. And we are all, before anything else human."
—Rob Bell

Remove all judgment and all shackles of doubt and enjoy this book as a book of stories from the old, the young, the middle-aged, and the ancient and, most importantly, from humans. Because that is what sex is about: humanity. So relax. It might get a little uncomfortable to talk about sex so openly but if you calm down there is a good chance you will enjoy this book and you may find yourself thinking, "Wow I didn't know that, tell me more."

I hope I touch your heart in a meaningful way and that you come out of the chapters exhilarated with more knowledge and wisdom.

Introduction

You are dressed in what seems like seven dresses. Your fingers are exposed even though you wear a pair of life-worn gloves. You are pushing an old shopping cart that testifies to the fact that it is your mobile home; you live at the mercy of elements. Your face shows the wear and tear due to years of living. You then bend over, looking through the garbage can, searching for life-sustaining remains discarded by the more fortunate society.

Suddenly, you shoot up out of the barrel and shout, "Found it! I found it!" There between your thumb and your index finger you hold the most beautiful pearl. People run over and ask you if they can help you. You smile and shake your head with a confidence that no-one expected in your status of life. Then you proceed to tell the people the story of your life that still impacts them up till today.

> *"And you shall know the truth and the truth shall set you free."*[1]

There are two things that come before freedom: knowledge and truth. It's one thing to want to be free but if you don't know the truth you will never be free. The problem is many some religious people are walking around claiming

---

1   John 8:32 [A Faithful Version]

freedom, singing about freedom, and wanting to be free but they are not honest. The truth is that sex is ravaging most of our lives and is one of the biggest things we deal with in life – whether or not it is talked about. Sexual urges, sexual frustrations, sexual ideas, and sexual partners; whether we do it or not, sex is one of the issues that everybody is dealing with.

I grew up in a fairly religious household, but I have had a very sour association with religion when it came to sex and sexual matters because the only thing they told us was, "Do not have it"! I feel that those who grew up outside of the church are at an advantage because they are not left with a question mark with regards to the topic of sex.

It was presented to me that sex was bad because it was something that I should not do; no one really dove deeper into the topic. The only instruction was to not have it! That was it! So what happens if you already did? What happens if – like in my case – you were sexually abused when you were a child? Or perhaps if you were raped? What happens if you were introduced to it in a locker room or a toilet by friends at school? What happens then?

Some religions (not all) stay away from the topic for various reasons. However this book tries to address the topic in an open unbiased way. Encouraging the reader to ask questions.

A study done by Gruber & Grupe states that 80% of children under the age of 16 are exposed to sexual images[2] and they were not taught about sex by parents, teachers, or pastors but instead were taught by social media, television, and friends who also have no clue what they are doing.

"Analyses of broadcast media content indicates that, on average, teenaged viewers see 143 incidents of sexual behavior on network television at prime time each week, with portrayals of three to four times as many sexual activities occurring between unmarried partners as between spouses. As much as 80% of all movies shown on network or cable television stations have sexual content. Analysis of music videos indicates that 60% portray sexual feelings and impulses, and a substantial minority display provocative clothing and sexually suggestive body movements. Analyses of media content also show that sexual messages on television are almost universally presented in a positive light, with little discussion of the potential risks of

---

2   Gruber & Grube (2000)

unprotected sexual intercourse and few portrayals of adverse consequences."[3]

Nearly half of US high school students will have sexual contact or relations before they finish their senior year, with African Americans significantly more likely to be sexually active (72%) than Hispanics (52%) or Whites (42%) – and this is just the average in the US, if you do more research on the topic you will find that other counties might have similar traits.

Sex is the essence of our lives but is it managed correctly? As a result, I am sharing with you things that I wish someone would have told me when I was younger. If I had been told what I know today it would have saved me a lot of heartache, pain, and soul searching. My whole life would have been different, but the beautiful thing is that I, and so many other people in this book, get to share our stories so that you have a fair chance of gaining knowledge and choosing which path you want to take in your life journey without bias or ignorance, but with wisdom and understanding. More importantly, with no doubt that SEX IS INDEED GOOD![4]

---

3   Gruber & Grube (2000).
4   Gruber & Grube (2000)

Before we continue, I have a question for you to consider: what is wisdom? Wisdom is when you receive knowledge from an external source like a book or a person, and then you take that knowledge and familiarise yourself with it. You then think about what the knowledge you got means to you. At this point, if it does not resonate you can chuck it away and forget about it, or you can take it in, analyse it, after which you get understanding, and after getting understanding you then do what it takes to apply what you have learnt. The application thereof is called wisdom.

I hope that you get wisdom from reading this book.

Chapter 1:
A MICROSCOPE ON RELIGION

The Collective Insanity

Let's start by looking at the word sin. Eckhart Tolle in his book, *A New Earth*, describes sin very eloquently: *"According to Christianity, the normal collective state of humanity is the "original sin". Sin is a word that has been greatly misunderstood and misinterpreted. Literally translated from the ancient Greek in which the new testament was written, to sin means to miss the mark as an anchor would miss the target., So to sin means to miss the point of human existence; it means to live unskilfully, blindly and thus suffer and cause suffering. Again, the term stripped of its cultural baggage and misinterpretations, points to the dysfunction inherent in the human being."* [5]

---

5   1 Tolle, E. (2005)

When it comes to sex we have all missed the mark. Religion has missed the mark by not giving clear guidance and information; They either have an implicit or a very explicit expectation, "Do not have sex". Society has missed the mark in keeping sex silent and at the same time vibrant, by dramatising it and creating ambiguity and illusive fantasies around it that normal humans can only dare to reach. Culture has missed the mark by normalising this silence and being shy on the topic. They have put fear around it and have made it seem as if it's okay to have sex as long as there are no conversations about it. Individuals have missed the mark by not informing themselves, not preparing themselves with a knowledge of sex, and by ignorantly having or not having sex out of peer pressure. They have succumbed to what they think is normal in their consciousness without digging deep to make informed decisions.

Unfortunately, the effects of talking too much and too little about sex are pretty much the same. While moralising explicitly reveals what activity is shameful, silence inspires the same shame but without all of the sexy details.

We have to understand that sex is inherent in creation and was not created by humans - we are all products of sex. The Bible offers the first instruction God gives humanity after blessing them in union: *"Then God blessed them (Adam and Eve) and said be fruitful and multiply."*[6] This was not an agricultural instruction. He made man, He made woman and He said, "Ey... you are naked and unashamed Adam. Do your thing and make sure you do it well." He told them that this is what He wanted them to do. That was the first command God gave to humanity: have sex! He did not tell them to go pray, He did not ask them to start planning; He said, "I want you to connect in intimacy and I want you to be fruitful and multiply."

This takes me to another text: *"But from the beginning of the creation God made them male and female."*[7] That means the Creator knows our parts, knows our desires, our urges, and our appetites. God is not thrown off by what you feel because He made you. Verse 7 of this same text goes on to say, *"This explains why a man leaves his father and mother and is joined to his wife."* [NLT] Now if we look at the word "joined", we most probably take it lightly. However, when you study the word in Hebrew it means to be yoked or attached. This

---

6   Genesis 1:28 [KJV, words in brackets added]

7   Mark 10:6-9 [KJV]

word can be extremely dangerous because it describes a 3-fold cord that takes place between 2 people. When you have sex, you are joined:

1) emotionally through intimacy,
2) physically through the act of sex, and
3) spiritually through covenant.

You might think it's a one-night stand but in reality, you are joining yourself to someone spiritually, physically, and emotionally, which poses a great danger and risk of what we call "soul ties".

What are soul ties? There are many definitions of soul ties and many different ways in which you can get soul-tied to another person or thing, but since we are talking about sex I find the following interpretation to be very true and profound. I can definitely attest to this definition because I have been there:

> *"A soul tie is the joining of one's essential self, mind, will, emotions, thoughts, and memories in connection to someone or something else."*[8]

---

8   http://www.bwcla.org/files/SOULTIES.pdf
     https://sadejheanell.medium.com/the-truth-about-soul-ties-bb4b2d2cdf1a

Let's look at a scriptural interpretation of a soul tie: *"Godly soul ties are formed when a couple are married (Ephesians 5:31, "For this cause shall a man leave his father and mother, and shall be joined unto his wife, and they two shall be one flesh."), and the Godly soul tie between a husband and the wife that God intended him to have is unbreakable by man (Mark 10:7-9). However, when a person has ungodly sexual relations with another person, an ungodly soul tie is then formed (1 Corinthians 6:16, "What? Know ye not that he which is joined to an harlot is one body? For two, saith he, shall be one flesh.").*[9]

This soul tie fragments the soul and is destructive. People who have many past relationships find it very difficult to 'bond' or be joined to anybody because their soul is fragmented"[10].

For example, you could have a one-night stand with a person who is suffering from anger or depression, and all of a sudden you start carrying the same emotional state as that person. Then you begin to question where the rage is coming from or why you're depressed. But what you do not realise is that it is a give-and-take emotional transfer. You might be doing something to fill a void but in reality what you are doing is

---

9   Kansema, J., (2020)

10   *Basic Introduction to Soul Ties*

creating a barrier to your future; every time you try to move forward something keeps holding you back.

People who have many past relationships find it very difficult to 'bond' or be joined to anybody, especially in marriage, because their soul is fragmented, tied to many different people. They partake in emotions that were absorbed through the engagement of sexual relationships that they should not have been a part of, for some this leads them in a downward spiral in all facets of life.

Sex has been so desensitised in this generation because we take it so lightly; we do not want to get to know people anymore, we just want to know what a person can do for us. In the Bible, marriage did not include certain rituals like having bridesmaids or groomsmen – that is what we do in these modern days. When God looks down and blesses the wedding it is when man and woman consummate the marriage (meaning, when they have sex). So when you have sex you are inviting the Spirit of the Creator to bless you in a covenant that creates a SOUL-TIE.

Sex was God's idea; it was not an invention of man. *"For this reason a man will leave his father and mother and be united to his wife, and the two will* *become **one flesh'**[a]? **6** So they are no longer two, but **one flesh**. Therefore what God has joined together, let no one separate. "*[11] His plan was of oneness: where everyone in this world would serve one God, and there would be one man with one woman. There would be one marriage with one sex partner; one flesh, one lifetime, with one picture.

Beyond a shadow of a doubt, the achievements of humanity are spectacular but we confuse the effects of tangible achievements with intangible ones. We have created sublime works of music, literature, painting, architecture, and sculptures. Also, science and technology have brought about radical changes in the way we live and have enabled us to do and create things that would have been considered supernatural a few decades ago. There is no doubt, the human mind is highly intelligent. Yet its very intelligence is tainted by madness. Human evolvement has magnified the destructive impact that the dysfunction of the human mind has upon the planet, other life forms, and humans themselves. If we were to examine history and previous generations when it comes to sex, we would be able to recognise something which Eckhart Tolle calls "the collective insanity".

---

11 Matthew 19:5-6 [NIV, emphasis added]

The Perversion of Sex

2nd Corinthians 6:9 states, -*"Don't you realise that this is not the way to live? Unjust people who don't care about God will not be joining in his kingdom. Those who use and abuse each other, **use and abuse sex,** use and abuse the earth and everything in it, don't qualify as citizens in God's kingdom."* [MSG, *emphasis added]*

The perversion of sex is nothing new. Here, according to scripture, Paul was talking to a group of people in Corinth who were living in the equivalent of modern-day Las-Vegas ("what happens in Vegas, stays in Vegas"). Corinth catered to lust and sexual sin and Paul was talking to people who were trying to come out of that lifestyle and trying to find out how to live in this sexually charged culture.

Does that not sound like today? Where we can literally wake up in the morning and scroll on our newsfeed then have an image implanted in our minds, or listen to a song which can stimulate and trigger different emotions including sexual.

Verse 11 then continues to say, *"A number of you know from experience what I'm talking about, for not so long ago you were on that list. Since then, you've been cleaned up and given a fresh start by Jesus, our Master, our Messiah, and by our God present in us, the Spirit." [MSG]*

The problem with us today is we try to hide the same thing that we do not want our children to suffer from. Whether it be parents, Pastors, or siblings: they will rarely come to you and say, "I have struggled with pornography, and a bad habit of sleeping around." This is because we do it in the dark and think that it's either natural or it will habitually go away. The sad thing is what you are suffering from may well be something that your children will suffer from too if you do not address it.

I was exposed to sex when I was 7 years old by a man who put his fingers in my vagina, and sexually harassed me. At that point I started groping through darkness. For the longest time, I lived in shame, fear, doubt, guilt, and agony. I was tainted, hurt and my innocence was stolen. In addition social media and TV which distorted my perspective. At some point I became sexually active which crippled my soul. Because I saw and experienced every man as a perpetrator, when I left the relationship a piece of me was ripped away. I was hopeless, senseless and lost. It was a difficult hurdle. But through conversations with people who allowed themselves to be humans. And through the pages of this book which took me almost a decade to complete I found grace.

The Sex Price Tag

"Because of the weakness of your human nature, I am using the illustration of slavery to help you understand all this. Previously, you let yourselves be slaves to impurity and lawlessness, which led ever deeper into sin. Now you must give yourselves to be slaves to righteous living so that you will become holy. When you were slaves to sin, you were free from the obligation to do right. And what was the result? You are now ashamed of the things you used to do, things that result in eternal doom. But now you are free from the power of sin and have become slaves of God. Now you do those things that lead to holiness and result in eternal life. For the wages of sin is death, but the free gift of God is eternal life through Christ Jesus our Lord." [Romans 6:19-23, NLT]

In this passage, Paul says that the wages of sin (missing the mark as discussed in a previous section) is death. What does this mean?

Let's start by explaining wages. Wages are a monetary reimbursement a person receives for the workings done over the course of some period of time. When Paul mentions death in this scripture, he is simply referring to spiritual death. Spiritual death is not something that happens at once but it's a gradual process that occurs in a person's soul who is involved in ongoing sin (**missing the mark**). The very fact that judgment is not quick and severe is part of the danger of it. The practice of sin brings death in small doses. With each indulgence comes a little more spiritual death of the soul; that is the payment deposited into one's account.

A few specific wages of missing the mark can be described as, but are not limited to:

Corruption

> *"For the secret power of lawlessness is already at work; but the one who now holds it back will continue to do so till he is taken out of the way."*
> 2 Thessalonians 2:7 [NIV]

Practicing "sin" in this case means consciously and constantly missing the mark, which sets off a mysterious operation that works on a person's heart and soul. It's like a virus that works its way into the deepest recesses of a person, corrupting everything it touches. The contaminating agent quietly, gradually, and unmeltingly alters one's soul into something crooked and bent. C.S. Lewis once said, "A bent hnau can do more evil than a broken one".

Sin drives a person into a frustrating life of dissatisfaction. It is a search or lust for an elusive fantasy that disappears right after you think you have received it. Every time you think about enjoying some tremendous degree of satisfaction over some sexual experience it vaporises and disappears. You are then left with nothing but the emptiness that sin always brings. As frustrating as this may be, the lust for these pleasures becomes so powerful that it keeps a person in a constant state of agitation for more. As soon as you are done with one empty fantasy, you are already chasing the next one. More frustration and more misery then follows; it's a never-ending cycle.

Self-centredness

The more you indulge in sin the more selfish you become. This is a process that happens gradually over some time; little by little the self-life grows and dominates your thinking. Before long the prevailing thought in your life becomes, "What is in it for me?" Decisions made throughout any given day go through that filter. Your gifts, intellect, wit, friendliness, leadership, memory, and much more are then all used to exalt your ego and please your self-life. Not knowing that selfishness is the very antithesis of true humanity.

Deadening of the Conscious

One of the biggest wages of missing the mark is the gradual loss of the ability to discern truth. This spiritual phenomenon is eloquently expressed by these men from the past:

> *"The most devastating effect of sin is that by it, we are blinded to it."* - Billy Graham

> *"Sin enough, and you will soon be unconscious of sin."* - Oswald Chambers

> *"You can sin yourself into an utter deadness of conscience and that is the first wage of your service of sin."* - Charles Spurgeon

God gave man a conscious as an inward monitor of the rightness and wrongness of his actions but over a period of time every new act of sin stifles the voice of consciousness a little bit more. It becomes seared and loses its ability to operate as the moral guardian of the soul. The fact is, a person cannot persist in habitual sin without hardening their hearts to the truth. Over time your perspective may become altered imperceptibly at first till a definite change begins to take place in you. Before you are aware of what is happening to you, right is seen as wrong, wisdom as foolishness, and good as evil.

As the heart becomes hardened it creates within a person a presumptuous attitude towards God. Professing Christians especially hold to the belief that they can turn to God whenever they are ready. They also insist that because they profess Christ, they can sin without any kind of judgement. What they do not realise is that the deeper they go into sin the stronger the illusion and the more presumptuous they become; the fear of God - the very thing that is greatly needed - becomes such a far away thought for such a person.

Misery

Solomon, in Proverbs 13:15 states that the way of the transgressor is difficult. The thing is, most of the time things seem to go wrong for the person in rebellion. The longer the practice of sin goes on, the worse the consequences become. Sin is death, hell, and misery to the soul. Avoid sin therefore as you would avoid misery.

Separation from the Fountain of Life

Furthermore, when engaging in sex outside of its original intention, the fountain is stopped, the flow of life is shut off, and the presence of God is withdrawn. It is like the story that narrates how every step a son and daughter take to a far-off country, takes them one step further away from the father's house. As they continue to move away from the house and its atmosphere, their perceptions, values, desires, and thinking change. Every step is transforming them into different people.

Most of the time a person has sex and they think they are done with it and forget about it. In reality, the energy never easily forgets you. There is within our being a recording mechanism that perfectly stores the memory of everything we have ever thought, said, or done. It's like a flight recorder that might be presented to you on judgement day.

There was research done on a man who was undergoing brain surgery and was kept awake during the procedure. The surgeons were trying to figure out which parts of the man's brain performed different functions, so they would press on one part and ask what he experienced. As they went through this procedure they started manipulating the part of his brain that stores memories. All of a sudden, long-lost memories flooded his mind so vividly that the man felt like he was living them right there on the spot.

This story reinforces that just because something was done in the past does not mean that the memories and effects of it are not still lodged within, but even more important is that it is being recorded in every aspect of your soul and sooner or later your secrets will find you out.

Sex and Choices

A definition of fear is the distressing emotion aroused by impending danger, whether the threat is real or imagined, but the church and religion insist that it only means having a reverence which is a misinterpretation of what it actually means. There is simply no beating around the bush when it comes to the fact that fear means fear. So many times Pastors and teachers of the bible talk about fearing the Lord and use it to deceive people. Fearing the Lord is more than just reverence; it is understanding that there is a Higher Power at play and that one needs to respect it just as you would the Law of Gravity.

The Law of Gravity, according to Newton, states: [12]

> *Every object in a state of uniform motion will remain in that state of motion unless an external force acts on it. Force equals mass times acceleration. For every action, there is an equal and opposite reaction. If you throw yourself from a skyscraper , you will die; there is no question or doubt about. If you are lucky you might damage a bone or two but it's very obvious that you will not survive because consequences are designed are built in.*

Unfortunately, that is how the universe works. In life, whatever decisions you make - good or bad - there are built-in consequences.

The Bible talks about adultery, fornication, and sexual immorality and calls them sin. For the

---

12   Editors of Encyclopaedia Britannica (n.d.)

longest time, I thought it was a pathetic joke. You mean all my desires and urges, I am supposed to suppress? For what? For whom? Why? "My body belongs to me, and I can do with it what I want", was my reaction. The thought of having some remote controller that I don't even know telling me, through the church, that I should not have sex was ridiculous and absurd.

"What is adultery anyway?" I asked myself as I researched: adultery really is about the violation of a relationship or violation of a contract. and what is fornication? I googled and got the following definition: "Fornication is generally consensual sexual intercourse between two people not married to each other."[13] Then I realised that the problem here was that adultery and premarital sex were being equated when in reality, they are two distinctly different things. I then found a verse written by Paul that seemed to suggest that sex between the unmarried is reprehensible . What??? "You must be crazy!" I thought to myself. But there it was:

> *"Now to the unmarried and the widows I say: It is good for them to stay unmarried, as I am. But*

---

13   Wikipedia online

if they cannot control themselves, they should marry, for it is better to marry than to burn with passion." [1 Corinthians 7:8-9, NIV]

At this time I had faced a lot of emotional pain because I had had different sexual partners that left me out to dry. I felt worthless and tainted; I hated men, and I was angry for what happened in my childhood. I did not trust, which caused a lot of confusion, mixed emotions, and wrong decisions. Using sex as an indulgence to make me feel better about myself but also as an unconscious tool of revenge, led to me unknowingly damaging myself even more. ,Reading a fancy scripture or even being told I was doing wrong resolved nothing, and so I continued until I met this one woman who told me her story, challenged me with rawness, and changed the trajectory of my life. .

It is important to note that the Bible consistently teaches self-control rather than self-indulgence. In Biblical teachings, the privilege of having sex requires the commitment of marriage. Sexually transmitted diseases, unintended pregnancy, and emotional pain are too often the price paid (the built-in consequence) for sex without marriage.

I then realised that this had nothing to do with religion and God: it was about me as an individual. People can talk and judge but until they step in my shoes they will never understand or even have the right to impose, "Do not have sex before marriage", without explaining their own history, and why they say so. There is nothing more deceiving than people who judge and tell you not to do certain things without taking you through a personal journey of how they found it to be true. There is power and a sense of attractiveness in honesty and truth but it has to be backed up by humility, non-judgment, and a genuine intention

There are many people who have the necessary information to change perceptions and help others but they remain silent because they are embarrassed, scared to be judged, confronted, or asked questions. But what if you were born for such a time as this? Instead of burying your past experiences, dig them out and show us how you survived or are surviving. Tell us why you say so, show us the scars so we can believe. Share your story and experiences without judgment or coercion but through passion and understanding. We need more people in churches who bare themselves than those who ignorantly speculate in the name of scripture and the Bible.

The problem that I found is that church people do not open up their wounds. Instead, they conceal them, hide in shame, and expect others to follow blindly. Unfortunately, the vagueness and broadness of the sexual constrictions in the purity movement left people confused, and often feeling that they must reject even normal healthy sexual urges. Sadly, only sexual urges within heterosexual, committed, adult relationships were defined as healthy. This leaves out a lot, and also abandons teens to feel unable to learn or understand their own sexual urges - with the notion that they will understand them once they're married.

Living Out My Choices

This is a story of a personal friend who dared to talk and helped shine a light in my life. Although experiences are different I found hope through her story.

After so much pain an suffering I reached a point where it was about me protecting myself and my character. I fell into a deep pit of insanity and depression, and even turned suicidal. I felt I had defiled the laws of gravity and continued digging my grave.

Years later, I was prepared and yearning for marriage, and I met this man whom I fell madly in love with. We eventually got married. I was 34 at the time and wanted children of my own, so we tried to fall pregnant. I cannot deny that the sex was amazing, but we could not conceive.

I then went to the doctor out of desperation; I remember that day as if it was yesterday. We had done our test beforehand and met with the doctor for the results. The doctor sitting before us was an old experienced man probably in his 40s. He looked at me and asked, "Would you like to talk about the results together?" I replied, "Yes, why not", seemingly worried about his question but hopeful nonetheless. This is what he said: "Ma'am you have Endometrial Cancer. You will not be able to conceive." I looked at my husband and his face dropped. I then tried to find composure and I asked the doctor why. I wanted to know what caused it. "I'm not sure of the causes ma'am. There are many theories like previous abortions and untreated STIs but we cannot say for certain."

My mind instantaneously took me back to all those abortions I had in the past. I thought of all the wasted years I spent not taking care of myself. Today we cannot have children of our own but when I look back at the scriptures that found me several years back *which I ignored bluntly, I realise that I cannot blame anyone else for where I stand today. In life, everything in this world is permissible but not all is beneficial.*

—Sandra Jones[*14]

---

14 * Name has been changed to protect the identity of the individual.

Chapter 2:
ADDICTION[15]

The human brain contains a vast system of nerves. Every thought or action a person engages in sends an electric pulse through those complex nerves. When the person starts repeating this behaviour those nerves become connected through a brain chemical known as a neurotransmitter. In essence, what happens is that the brain creates pathways which these chemical signals can travel on. Think of a field of weeds and brush between two villages; over time people walking through these villages develop a trail that becomes wider, smoother, and easier to walk on. In a similar fashion, that is how we were created to form a habit in our brains.

Habits are extremely important to us as human beings because they allow our bodies to function effectively. Think about what it would

---

15   Chapter inspired by Horvath et al (n.d.)

be like if we had not developed a habit of walking, eating, typing, etc. By increasing the behaviour we become increasingly more proficient at certain things until it becomes second nature to us. This is made possible because of the pathways those neurotransmitters travel on.

One of the most important neurotransmitters the brain produces is called Dopamine. It's classified as the feel-good hormone because it's associated with the motivation to repeat pleasurable experiences. This is how God established within us the desire to eat and to procreate. When a person enjoys some small pleasure in life such as eating a piece of chocolate or watching a favourite movie, a small amount of dopamine is released in the person's brain. Like other neurotransmitters, dopamine moves through the nerve highways. However, dopamine is different because the amount that is released through the nerve centre is dependant on the level of pleasure that was just experienced.

Extreme examples would be the first time a person snorts cocaine or ejaculates. That level of intense pleasure causes a powerful surge of dopamine to flood the brain. For instance, it might take a young person weeks to get into the habit of brushing their teeth but it may only take days to establish a powerful habit of masturbation. That is because the high surge release of dopamine quickly creates a mental highway for impulses to travel on. As a person repeats this pleasurable experience that produces this rush of dopamine, it quickly creates a shortcut highway through the brain system. Dopamine does not only contribute to the sense of pleasure but also plays a crucial role in learning and memory - two key elements in the transition from liking something to becoming addicted to it.

The psychological effects of this rush of dopamine are so powerful that sights, sounds, and even smells present during the experience can produce a lifelong association with that experience. The sense of smell is especially susceptible to this phenomenon. Think of a person who is addicted to food trying to lose weight; just a whiff of their favourite food can take them on a rollercoaster ride back to their old habits. Eating is not the factor but the abuse of food is the main problem, just as sex is not the problem but the abuse of it is. According to the Mental Health and Substance Abuse Clinic, Gulf Bend Center[16], because sex is an activity that

---

16   Horvath et al (n.d.)

promotes the survival of the species, the brain rewards this activity differently creating a pleasurable feeling which makes humans more vulnerable to addiction.

The article goes on to state, *"People are not addicted to sex. As with all addictions, people become addicted to the brain chemicals released during the substance use or activity (in this case, sex), not the substance or activity itself."* It all starts somewhere where you want more and more, and your receptors get weaker and weaker that you are no longer easily satisfied. We were created to indulge in beautiful experiences but with discipline and control. Due to a lack of control, the brain receptors become overwhelmed, so the brain compensates for this by producing less dopamine as these chemical surges continue. Over time every new sexual encounter brings about a decrease in the euphoric sensation that dopamine produces. It is the scientific reality of what is behind the principle of the diminishing marginal rate of utility. What begins as an exhilarating experience eventually loses its luster. This drop in the level of dopamine also leads to a physical, emotional, and spiritual crash, which in turn brings about feelings of depression.

So what does the addict do? They return to the same old behaviour hoping for the intense pleasure and euphoria they experienced earlier. Unfortunately, this cycle of the high of pleasure and the subsequent effects of the emotional crash deepens the brain pathways. Over time the person goes from repeating behaviour because of the pleasure of it, to doing it because he needs it. When the craving becomes more intense than ever while the actual pleasure enjoyed becomes minimal, the habit has crossed the line into an addiction.

True Story: Chronicles of a man who was caught in the clenches of addiction

I grew up in a very unstable environment; the biggest problem was that my father was extremely self-centred and simply lacked the capacity to love others. I suppose it's the lack of love in our home that created a void in my heart and I did the same thing countless others have done: I tried to fill that emptiness with material things.

A healthy home is built on a solid foundation of empathy, affection, understanding, discipline, and love. These are some of the important character traits that were missing in my household growing up. My dad's behaviour caused a breach in our relationship which he tried to make up for by buying me things and then disciplining me in an inconsistent and abusive way. I sought comfort in material things and it did not take me long to figure out how to avoid his temper and manipulate him into buying me what I wanted. He was the type of person that was rebellious in nature, causing harm towards himself and others. When he was irritated by anything and nothing, he would strike out in anger and abuse towards everyone around him.

I already knew the routine: irritate my dad which would lead to him being violent and abusive. After a while, he would feel guilty which would result in him buying me what I wanted - the latest toys and games. He was emotionally unstable and yet it worked for me because of how predictable he was. As I reached my teen years my mentality shifted from possessions (that is, getting stuff like toys and games) to experiences such as sex and drugs. I would do anything for what I wanted as I would weigh the punishment against the fulfilment. What I did not know was that this world that I had created led me to become an increasingly selfish and self-centred monster. Sex became the great passion of my life; a daily fair of pornography and masturbation kept me locked in my room for days where no-one else could intrude. The natural ability I *had for seducing girls allowed me to selfishly entice and dump them when I was done. But it was my discovery of hardcore pornography that set me on an obsessive path where I came to the place bordering on the edge of insanity.*

It was self-centeredness that led me into addiction in the first place but pursuing the sexual behaviours only exacerbated my selfishness. Sex was the primary focus of my attention but of course, there were other aspects to life as well which, to be honest, were overshadowed by this desire. I went after whatever I wanted with little regard to how it might affect other people, and if anyone stood in my way I became irritated and angry. Interestingly the more I got what I desired and the more I got what I wanted, the more miserable I became. The more I gave the monster of self what it demanded the greater it became within me. My life eventually came to a point where it was one big dark cloud of self; there was no room for anyone else. Self demanded and received nearly everything it wanted.

CS Lewis once said, "We must picture hell as a state where everyone is perpetually concerned with his own dignity and advancement, where everyone has a grievance and where everyone lives with the deadly serious passions of envy, self-importance, and resentment."[17] *The selfishness that this statement depicts sums up the black hole my life became.*

Through different encounters, and with difficulty, I eventually turned my life around, but it took me a while to understand that there is a life based on selflessness rather than selfishness; it is founded on humility, not pride. I tried to seek this through religion but I did not find it. Instead, I found it in the most amazing of places which was the canvass of a relationship with my Creator. Roy Hession said, "It is so often self who tries to live the Christian life... It is always self who gets irritable and envious and resentful and critical and worried. It is self who is hard and unyielding in its attitudes to others. It is self who is shy and self-conscious and reserved."[18] *And so the story goes, I am not perfect but, as Tonny Robbins put it, "Only those who have learned the power of sincere and selfless contribution experience life's deepest joy: true fulfilment".*

—*Paul Junior**[19]

---

17 Lewis, C.S. (1942)

18 Hession, R., (n.d.)s

19 * Name has been changed to protect the identity of the individual.

Chapter 3:
TABOO

Let's talk about sex, baby (sing it)
Let's talk about you and me (sing it, sing it)
Let's talk about all the good things
And the bad things that may be
Let's talk about sex (come on)
Let's talk about sex (do it)
Let's talk about sex (uh-huh)
Let's talk about sex
Ladies, all the ladies, louder now, help me out
Come on, all the ladies — let's talk about sex, all
right[20]

In 1991, whether they realised it or not, the all-female group Salt-N-Pepa would leave a lasting impression on the minds of listeners everywhere with their smash hit "Let's Talk About Sex." This was not necessarily because of the groove or the danceability of the song, but

---

20   Lyrics taken from the song **Let's Talk About Sex** performed by Salt-N-Pepa (1991)

rather because the song opened a dialogue with millions of listeners across the globe. Their message? You have to talk about sex. You have to discuss the bad and the good in order to make it work.

And then there were the *50 Shades of Grey* trilogies! Oh, what a wealthy woman I would be if I had a dime for every person I met who uttered "50 Shades" with pure, unadulterated delight. Actually, the only thing that would surpass that financial windfall would be the number of times people acted awkwardly, in silence and sheer horror, looking ashamed, or giggling at the very mention of anything to do with sex. The ability to engage in open communication about sex is an area that still remains taboo throughout society today.

What is interesting is that sex has long been a topic cloaked in fantasy, privacy, and kept between the sheets of consenting adults. That is, unless you look into any mainstream media. Society might have you believe that sex not only sells but that it should be something that comes easy to anyone engaged in the conversation. Advertisers guarantee your sexual attraction if you just buy their product. Modern-day fiction plays out sexual scenarios many only dare fantasise about. These are the kinds of desires we dare not utter in public - or in private, for that matter. The "sex sells" trend doesn't seem to be reversing anytime soon. One has only to look at the capital being dumped into this industry.

Sex and romance are noted as some of the largest income generators in any industry. Have you considered buying a steamy novel? Apparently, so has everyone else. The romance fiction industry is worth over a billion dollars. Wondered whether you should spice up your sex life with toys? In 2017, the global markets for the adult industry reported a net worth of close to $23.7 billion dollars.[21] Additionally, these figures were projected to increase by about 40 percent by 2020. Add in the income of the porn industry and we can pay off the debts of, and feed, small countries... for life. We have made it a curiosity; we love to watch, read about, and participate in sex - but with all this interest and openness about it, why do we struggle to speak about it openly?

---

21   Business Wire online (October, 2018)

Parents & Trust

True Story: How I Stumbled Upon Sex

When I was 15 I had an epic experience in the bathroom. I was taking a bath, then suddenly I found myself rubbing against my leg. It felt a little ticklish but very good so I continued unto the feeling. At some point, it got very intense and felt as though something wanted to burst out of me. I was not sure what was happening, but it felt so good and eventually I had a gush of sperm come out of me. It was the first time I had seen such, so I was somewhat embarrassed. The sperm filled the bathtub with white goo and I quickly had to clean it because I thought to myself, "My parents cannot see this".

When I think about it today I could not explain why I was embarrassed but it just felt wrong. From that day I was very intrigued by this and continued exploring. This was 1992, and in those days we did not have much technology so we used to exchange discs via post. How this worked is that people would write a classified in the local newspaper stating that they were interested in exchanging discs, and they would include their contacts and home address. Most of the time we would exchange good pictures and music with unknown people, but on this particular day, a scallywag sent me semi porn and nude pictures. Those blew me away!

The pictures were very subtle and elusive, unlike those we see today; back then it was the best we could get. Those kept me entertained for hours and my parents never noticed neither did they mention anything that had to do with sex. I then started hearing more about it. I remember the first time I heard it spoken about was in the school locker room where my friends were discussing how it was actually done. I never tried having sex with a woman till I was 20 and when I did it was the most embarrassing, bizarre moment of my life. I wish that my dad had sat me down and explained what sex is, and talked me through it. It would have saved me a world of trouble.

—J. Phillips*[22]

True Story: How I Impacted My Driver

Haviing the knowledge my mom gave me allowed me to be a trusted sounding board and support to many of my friends who didn't have adults talking to them. It wasn't just peers that I had the ability to educate. A few months ago, while taking an Uber home

---

22 * Name has been changed to protect the identity of the individual.

from the movie theater, I started talking to the driver and found out that he had two teen daughters, one of which is going off to college next year. I began telling him about the benefits of talking about sex. I told him my mum was an anchor for me in the way she approached the topic and I shared what she taught me with him. He then asked, "What does your mom do for a living?", out of sheer curiosity as if to say, "Wow! Where and how did she learn to talk about such topics with her children so boldly?" He became even more interested when I told him she was a caterer and he really wanted to deep dive into this topic to know how to talk to his daughter about sex before she left for college. With boldness, I told him all I know.

He told me that he knew he should say something, but that he was afraid because he didn't know how to approach the subject. He said he grew up in Africa where talking about sex is very taboo. I then started to explain the importance of having these conversations to prevent rape and sexual abuse; that it's all about self-love, as well as love and respect for others, rather than it being about trying to corral her from having sex. I witnessed a light bulb go off in his head. It was clear to me that my efforts to shift his perspective for the betterment of his daughter's well being had worked. He finished the conversation by thanking me immensely for all of my help. Without my sex-positive upbringing, I know that interaction would not have been possible. Without having grown up in a sex-positive way, I believe so many of my experiences would have turned out very differently. I'm much more confident and prepared to pursue exactly what I want related to my body and pleasure without any shame.

—*Petra Motaung*[23]

The benefits of parents having sexual health conversations with their children, as they grow, reach far beyond whether and when they have sex. Even if it's uncomfortable, it's important that children know their parent is someone they can turn to and trust for talks like this. I hope these tidbits of my experiences motivate parents to get vulnerable with their kids and start, or continue, having the talks that support their sexual health.

In moments of difficulty, having a support system can help keep us from falling apart. As kids, whenever something went wrong or we were faced with fear we'd rely on our parents for support. These moments with our parents are what made our relationship as daughter/son flow in calm waters. However, as we get older there

---

23   Name has been changed to protect the identity of the individual.

are many new experiences that we explore that can cause problems if one is not safe, especially when it comes to sex.

Talking to our parents about sex can get really awkward but that doesn't mean that they need to know everything that you do that's sex-related. As an example, what about when you've gone a month without a period and you've gotten tested but they all come out negative. What then? You're probably losing your senses and don't know what to do. During moments like this, you're looking for support and advice but don't want to ask your parents because they might not trust you anymore… Why is this? Are our parents not there to support us?

Everyone's parents are different. For most parents the approach of "sex silence" became a rule. We have a society that just gets prude about the topic of sex. **It seems as though our generation's taboo is the fear of talking about sex**. Foucault, on the history of sex, tells us that, *"Nothing that was not ordered in terms of generation or transfigured by it could expect sanction or protection. Nor did it merit a hearing. [The subject of sex] would be driven out, denied, and reduced to silence. Not only did it not exist, it had no right to* *exist and would be made to disappear upon its least manifestation - whether in acts or in words."*[24]

Sure this was a major issue back in the '70s but this view still floats around amongst today's generation. Instead of asking our parents about an issue relating to sex, we choose to remain silent, and instead seek indirect communication from the internet to find our answers. What you do in the bedroom should be kept to yourself and your partner, but what happens when one gets some type of infection or something goes wrong? Surely we can talk to our partner about it, right? That comforting support from our parents is what we yearn for most yet it is difficult to break through the walls of silence and unnecessary embarrassment.

Sex is something that we all do at some point in our life. We cannot free ourselves from this sort of repression simply by means of theory: we must learn to be more open about our sexuality; to talk about it, to enjoy it! Ignorance is not bliss when it comes to these topics. Some parents feel that if they do not talk about it, it will just go away or not happen. The sad truth is if you leave your child exposed and naked to the ideologies

---

24   Foucault, (1976)

of different people who have had different experiences, it sets a foundation for confusion. This can haunt you as a parent, or if you are lucky enough, it might only affect the child at a later stage. Why not address it before? Set a foundation.

The Role of Religion in Making Sex a Taboo Topic

It is certainly interesting and legitimate to ask why sex has been associated with sin for such a long time. It would remain to be discovered how this association was formed, although with that being said one should be careful not to state in summary or hasty fashion that sex is "condemned". If we look clearly in Christianity, Hinduism, Islam, Jainism, or any other religion, is it honourably stated - explicitly or implicitly - that sex is sin? We should ask ourselves what paths have brought us to a point where we are at fault with respect to our own sexuality.

Yes, sex before marriage, also known as adultery, might be considered a sin depending on your beliefs, but SEX in itself is not a sin. Religion has used this as a form of repression to suppress and discourage. Suppression and discouragement without true understanding lead to indecent behaviour and rebellion. We have become a civilisation so peculiar that we fall prey to the abuse of power by religion or religious leaders. We fail to rationalise our own thoughts as to what sex really is. We have been led blindly, implicitly, and unconsciously for years. It is sad but true that many people today subconsciously affirm this repression because it is firmly anchored; it has solid roots and reasons which weigh so heavily on the topic of sex that more than one denunciation will be required to free ourselves from it.

Culture and Sexual Repression

The repression that has been stated above feeds into society and becomes the norm; it's a chain reaction. Foucault describes it very well in his study, ***The History of Sexuality (Volume 1)***:

"For a long time, the story goes, we supported a Victorian regime, and we continue to be dominated by it even today. Thus the image of the imperial prude is emblazoned on our restrained, mute, and hypocritical sexuality. At the beginning of the seventeenth century a certain frankness was still common, it would seem. Sexual practices had little need of secrecy; words were said without undue reticence, and things were done

without too much concealment; one had a tolerant familiarity with the illicit." [page 3]

Foucault, through his research, realised - and was describing - how sex had changed and how the perception of it had changed from what it was then to what it became in the nineteenth century. He mentions that the 17th century was a time of direct gestures; people had no shame and were free-spirited when it came to sex and sexual matters. Children were amongst adults where they were able to learn from them and be educated about sex without embarrassment or discomfort.

From the nineteenth century, everything changed slowly but surely. People became more confined and secretive with regards to sex instead of it being spoken of freely. Sex became confined to the bedroom and locked among its walls. This is when society started to be misled and this dilemma continues to this day. We have no problem with locking the doors to sexual matters and dealing with the issues that arise from it in the dark. This is certainly not to say have sex in the public square and start shouting, "Hey come look! I'm having sex!" No, far from it! But it's about living a life without being embarrassed to discuss sexual health, wellbeing, and the issues arising from sexual encounters between the young and old, because the key to sexual freedom is communication. It's about opening up our hearts and minds to find knowledge from each other and about learning from one another, which will, in turn, change the perception of society on the issue of sex.

We live in a sexually charged world where illicit and unrealistic expectations are portrayed to us every day. As a result, we face so much emotional pain and shame when it comes to such matters. There are not enough people who are willing to break the chains, break the silence, and shed some light on the topic. But then again it could be a case of us having been corrupted by the change of season and time so that we look at sex through the veil of ignorance. A good example would be the fact that we are all aware that children are not supposed to have sex so we hide it from them, silently declaring it as impermissible. We then close our eyes and pretend not to know when the evidence points to the contrary; declaring an injunction to silence, an affirmation of nonexistence, and, by tacit implication, a surrender like the Japanese pictorial maxim - "see no evil, hear no evil, speak no evil".

We indirectly declare that there is nothing to say about such things, nothing to see, and nothing to know. Such is the hypocrisy of our orthodox society with its distorted logic. It is forced to make a few concessions, however, only if it is truly necessary to make room for illegitimate sexualities. Brothels, prostitution, the client, and the pimp, are all tolerated in this regime. Words and gesticulations can be exchanged here at the offer rate, and only in these places can pleasures and experiences be traded from one to another. Only in these places will you hear of stories of how one friend recommends another to the hottest fille de joie in the bar and how exciting it was the night before. Everywhere else it is considered a taboo. Sound familiar? We have subjected ourselves to societal and cultural norms that are hypocritical in nature, but of course, they have deep roots in the past.

Chapter 4:
SELF-ESTEEM

True Story: Jane The Virgin*[25]

I lost my virginity under the starry sky. We were laying outside a tightly built house close to the living room window. We had a brown drugget on the floor and we were cosily staring at the night sky. He knew I was a virgin, I think he was too but I'm not certain. We started touching each other, his finger slid down and I tried to make him stop - not hard enough though. Soon we were so overwhelmed by the feeling of passion that we ended up lying naked on top of each other. My mind was running with questions like, "What if his parents hear us?" The house was tiny and all the rooms were so connected that you could hear every sound. "What if they find out? Am I ready?"

As my mind was buzzing, I felt a deep penetration, and then it stopped. I thought to myself, "What just

---

25 * Name has been changed to protect the identity of the individual.

happened?" I asked him, "Is that it?" He said, "Yes!" I breathed deeply and thought, "Wow that was not what I expected." We picked up the mat and snuck back inside the house through the narrow door and went into the confined room which had double beds stacked on top of each other for children. On the bottom bed lay his brother sleeping, so we tried by all means not to wake him as we went to the upper bed. It was not my assigned room so we set an alarm for 2 hours of sleep so that I could then move to the visitor's room.

We tried again to penetrate and the same thing happened so we slept. When we woke up the bed was full of blood. He was so sweet about it and he apologised, took the sheets, and washed them. I sheepishly went to my room. He then came and lay next to me in the visitor's room till morning. When his mother woke up she came into the room and saw us. I sneaked my eyes open as she held her mouth in surprise and withdrew as if she saw nothing. I immediately shoved him over so that he could wake up and leave. That is how our secret was uncovered. After some time I confessed to my parents. They were very disappointed but I felt it was my time to break the rules - biggest mistake of my life!

We decided that we were going to live together fresh out of high school. I applied for a job and went to *the city of gold. He joined me and we lived together. He was not working so I had to support him; it was exciting times but also tough times for both of us. As couples do, we tried having sex but he could not get hard. Unfortunately, what I experienced when losing my virginity ended up being a lifelong challenge. We did so many things to try and help him. I was there for him through it all so much that it drained my energy; I could have probably still been there had it not been for the abuse. He beat me up to a pulp whenever he could. I understand now that it was because of his frustration with being a man who was unable to give pleasure. I had patience with him but it ran dry.*

We decided to visit his parents at some stage. I had a friend who lived not so far from their house who had always fancied me. One day I decided to create drama and became upset so that I could storm out and visit this friend of mine. I had sex with him and for the first time, it felt glorious. However, I felt guilty halfway through and stormed out, leaving the poor man hanging. My boyfriend at that time lacked confidence, self-esteem, and love. He was young, did not have a job but rushed out to come live with me. I also should have been in university and done better but I decided to flee from my parent's home for the sake of love.

I was 19 at that time and I still needed to mature and learn to deal with situations that were complicated. Because I was in a rush it, in turn, fostered low self-esteem, pity, and shame within me. I could not tell anyone about my issues because I had made a choice that was unfavourable. I stayed in this sour relationship of abuse, shame, and lack of love for 8 years. Feeling nothing but poor and broken down, my boyfriend also felt the same but we could not let each other go because of self-pity towards ourselves and each other.

I started cheating out of emptiness and he too tried to test his capabilities only to find out that we were both still feeling worthless as we were feeding off each other. I had measured my self-worth through the lens of my boyfriend; I had concluded that there was nothing better and that I was supposed to take care of him because he was struggling. I took on issues and problems that were too big for my shoes. I was young and naïve, and I stepped on dangerous ground before my time. As a result, the emptiness overflowed in my conversations, thoughts, soul, and into my heart until eventually, it manifested into breast cancer. I had to go for an operation, and my doctor - who was very much in touch with his spirit - explained his theory and said cancer is a black nuclear cell that develops in the body due to stress and anxiety. Of course he was just talking non-proven theories but at that point in time, I decided

I needed to end the relationship and that was the beginning of my life.

—*Jane*[*][26]

Self-esteem is described as the evaluation of one's self; how a person views him/herself in any situation. There was a study done in Nigeria [27]where they were trying to assess the relationship between low- and high self-esteem with sex and risky behaviour. They had 169 male participants and 192 female participants of a minimum age of 16.9 years. The study showed that adolescents with low self-esteem had a high score on the Beck Hopelessness Scale (BHS), which is based on self-esteem categories, and were more likely to be sexually active and show risky behaviour compared to those with higher self-esteem.

What is interesting is that the idea of sex and self-esteem is two-fold; you can have low self-esteem and want to use sex to gain power and approval from others or you can have low self-esteem and shy away from sex. Either way, just like the story above, sex and matters concerning sex can shape the outcome of how you see

---

26 * Name has been changed to protect the identity of the individual.

27 Enejoh, V. et al (2015)

yourself going forward. Fortunately, or unfortunately, sex and how you view yourself matters as that is what will guide you.

Chapter 5:
SEX: A GOOD IDEA

Having sex isn't just a sure-fire way to feel closer to your partner and enjoy some time connecting with your own body, but sex also has some pretty powerful benefits for your mental health[28].

1. Sex Gives You a High

    The pleasure you feel during sex is largely due to dopamine. As discussed in Chapter 2, dopamine is associated with feelings of euphoria, bliss, motivation, and concentration.[29]

2. Sex is an Antidepressant

    During sex, your brain produces several chemicals and hormones that help you feel satisfied, relaxed, and in a better mood. One study noted that women who had sex without

---

28   Giuliano, F. (2011)
29   Gynecol, W.J.O. (2018)

a condom had fewer depressive symptoms than women who used a condom. The researchers hypothesised that compounds in semen, including estrogen and prostaglandin, have antidepressant properties. This is good news for anyone who is in a committed relationship, but if you're not monogamous, it's not worth giving up condoms.[30]

3. Sex Improves Memory

One study found that sex increases cell growth in the hippocampus in rodents. The hippocampus is a brain region crucial to long-term memory. The experiment discovered that, when compared with rats who were only allowed a one-night stand, rodents who engaged in "chronic" sexual activity grew more neurons in the hippocampus. The findings were repeated in a second experiment with mice. It isn't known if more sex has the same effect on humans, but you can always operate on the premise that it does.[31][32]

4. Sex is a Stress Reliever

Science suggests that sex can improve your mood and decrease anxiety by reducing stress

30   Vann, M.R. (2011)

31   Leuner, B., Glasper, E.R., & Gould, E. (2010)

32   Dodgson, L. (2018)

signals in the brain and lowering blood pressure. It works conversely too. Sexual interaction and physical affection improve mood and reduce stress, and improved mood and reduced stress increase the likelihood of future sex and physical affection in a relationship. It's a win/win![33]

5. Sex is a Sleep Aid

   Good news for insomniacs: sex can make it easier to fall asleep, and increased amounts of sleep help boost your sex drive. Another win/win. The sleepy effect is due to the hormones released. Additionally, having an orgasm releases another hormone, prolactin, which makes you relaxed and sleepy. Getting physical is more likely to induce sleep in men than women because the prefrontal cortex of a man's brain slows down after ejaculation. When combined with the hormone surges, this can result in the well-known "rolling over and falling asleep" behavior.[34]

6. Sex Makes You Smarter

   In one study, researchers found that people who indulged in frequent, regular sexual activity scored higher on an array of mental

---

33 Burleson, M.H., Trevathan, W.R., & Todd, M. (2006)

34 Krans, B. (2019)r

tests:[35]

- Their verbal fluency was better.
- Their ability to visually perceive objects was improved.
- They could judge the space between objects better.

There are four phases to the sexual response cycle:

1. Excitement
2. Plateau
3. Orgasm
4. Resolution

Excitement

In this initial stage of arousal, serotonin is released; a neuron transmitter that causes you to feel happy. When you get excited or aroused your pupils dilate - a sign that your nervous system is working at increasing levels. Adrenaline is released, the heart rate starts accelerating, blood rushes to the genitals, and in the woman's case, to her clitoris and labia minora. The man's penis becomes erect. Men experience a tightening

---

35   Clarke, M. (n.d.)

of the scrotum, swelling of the testicles, and a discharge of liquid meant to lubricate. Women also begin lubrication, and dopamine is released which increases the sexual desire. Everything that is experienced begins to intensify; this is now the Plateau.

Plateau

Continuing on from the initial excitement of your increased heart rate, muscle tension and blood pressure rise. Norepinephrine is released during stimulation making your special areas more sensitive; muscles in the feet, face, and hands may begin to spasm.

Orgasm

The pelvic muscles contract, a woman's uterus and the base of a man's penis experience rhythmic contractions. The heavy amounts of ejaculation, together with the nerves that have been built up, release everything involuntarily at once in the form of intensely pleasurable weights. Males ejaculate their semen, females may experience ejaculation as well, and the oxytocin level - or the love hormone - peaks at orgasm. This is where, researchers argue, possibly trust and closeness between partners is built.

Resolution

Sexual arousal usually decreases, the contraction and swelling subside, and some women may be able to return to the orgasm phase. However, men go into a refractory period, a time where they cannot yet reach the orgasm phase, so they just wait it out. The cycle of pleasure continues.

We Have One Rule

I totally love sex; it builds a bond of intimacy that is tight. I was born to have sex - no doubt about it. Everyone is, but sometimes really to be honest I don't feel like it. My husband wants it all the time - he is more like a sex machine - but I have succeeded (partially) in making him understand that as a woman, I have cycles. There is summer when I just want to be touched in all the right places; autumn when it is just windy; spring when all is colourful and fun and I start opening up; and then winter where I don't want to be touched.

Sex is beautiful and is good for procreation too. I am planning to have children in the near future but for now, we are both just enjoying the ride. The first time I had sex though it was not what I expected. Now because I love and trust my partner, we can talk about various positions and how we can satisfy each other. He is still a little shy to talk about it but he has come a long way to become comfortable with it. I have found that talking about sex in our relationship has built a pillar of comfort and love between us. We have a rule that we live by when it comes to sex: Don't make me feel bad for asking and I will not make you feel bad for saying no!

Chapter 6:
SEX DIARIES

*T*he interviews you are about to read were conducted on a host of people from around the world who participated in sharing their story. Interviews were conducted either face-to-face or via Survey Monkey online. The names of participants have been left out in a bid to protect their identities. The diaries were formulated from surveys and live interactions over a period of 3 years, from 2018 to 2020.

The Single's Diary

As we dive into the mind and thoughts of the single population, it's interesting to note the similarities as well as the differences between the males and females.

. . . .

"I am almost always drunk."

Age: Undisclosed
Identifies as: Female
Has sex with: Men

How many people have you had sex with recently?

"Since getting out of a long-term relationship a year and a half ago, five."

How often do you have sex?

"Once a week for a few weeks when I'm seeing someone...which is every few months."

How do you meet the people you're sleeping with?

"Mutual friends/Tinder."

Describe your sex life.

"Couple sex was almost always sober; single sex is almost always drunk. I'm actually not usually that interested in sex until I'm more familiar with someone, because I don't feel comfortable being naked with a complete stranger. Single sex is definitely more exciting. Couple sex can get stale unless you really work hard at [it]... The best thing about being single is being able to do what you want, when you want, and not feeling obligated to spend your nights/weekends with someone."

"I can end up feeling insecure and depressed."

Age: 27
Identifies as: Female
Has sex with: Men

How many people have you had sex with recently?
"Two."

How often do you have sex?
"Twice a week."

How do you meet the people you're sleeping with?
"Friends, mainly. I am not into casual sex at all. The emotional connection is not there with casual sex, which makes it very hard to relax and enjoy the experience. When I have casual sex or a one-night stand, I end up feeling insecure and depressed about how I could give my body away so easily."

"I like that it is protected sex and involves no babies."

Age: 30
Identifies as: Male
Has sex with: Women

How many people have you had sex with recently?
"I banged 27 girls last summer."

How often do you have sex?
"An average of 16 times a year."

How do you meet the people you're sleeping with?
"I've met people I've slept with online, in bars, parks, college campuses, grocery stores, buses, hardware stores, arts and craft stores, malls, fast-food chains, libraries, bathrooms, and eBay."

Describe your sex life.
"Casual sex is fulfilling, not routine. My favorite thing about single sex is that it's protected — no babies."

"I try to be non-judgmental."

Age: 24
Identifies as: Male
Has sex with: Men

How many people have you had sex with recently?

"Probably four in the last month."

How often do you have sex?

"Four times a month."

How do you meet the people you're sleeping with?

"Different sites online. OKCupid, Craigslist - not Grindr. I like the concept of exploring sex as divorced from emotional connection. That's not to say I don't enjoy sex in a monogamous relationship. But, I've found that single sex has allowed me to deal with my inhibitions and hangups and learn to just be, to enjoy physical contact with another person in a way that I've never been able to before. I have more agency now, and I know what I want and I go after it. I try to be non-judgmental — especially since I do this often. As someone who's had a lot of meaningful, monogamous sex, as well as single sex, I think that while they're completely different experiences, neither one is better than the other — and no one should be shamed for engaging in either."

....

"I'm all in favor of casual sex in theory but tend to find it unsatisfying."

Age: 29
Identifies as: Female
Has sex with: Men

How many people have you had sex with recently?
"One in the past year."

How often do you have sex?
"A couple of times per year, generally."

How do you meet the people you're sleeping with?
"They tend to be friends first. I'm all in favor of casual sex in theory but tend to find it unsatisfying. It's less emotionally intimate; it can be hotter or can be just awkward. I like not having my sex life dictated by another person's desires (in my last relationship, my ex wanted it much more often than I did)."

"I almost always need to have a drink before having casual sex."

Age: 28
Identifies as: Male
Has sex with: Women

How many people have you had sex with recently?
"This year to date, two."

How often do you have sex?
"Eight times per month."

How do you meet the people you're sleeping with?
"JDate. I'm over casual sex; I'm 28. I almost always need to have a drink before having casual sex. When I'm part of a couple, I know what she likes — and a mutual orgasm is obviously better."

"Single sex can be a lot more selfish."

Age: 26
Identifies as: Female
Has sex with: Men

How many people have you had sex with recently?
"In 2014, I've had sex with five people, two

of whom were people I've slept with repeatedly in the past."

How often do you have sex?
"It varies depending on who's in the picture — typically at least once a week."

How do you meet the people you're sleeping with?
"I've met people through friends, out at the bar, and most recently, through Tinder."

Describe your sex life.
"Single sex can be a lot more selfish, especially during one-night stands. I have a lot fewer inhibitions with someone I won't ever see again. Having been single more often than not in the last five years, a lot of the sex I'm having is made up of casual sex and one-night stands."

"I want to have more sex."

Age: 28
Identifies as: Female
Has sex with: Men

How many people have you had sex with recently?
"One - we are in a long-term relationship."

How often do you have sex?
"Twice a week."

How do you meet the people you are sleeping with?
"Oh, I met him at a hotdog stand."

Describe your sex life.
"Intimate, exploratory but minimal. I would certainly like to have sex more often than twice a week :) Almost all of my relationships began with casual sex. I love being able to sleep with different people — the variety in my sex life is unmatched by monogamous sex. As much as I love being in a relationship, it's a lot easier to be in a rut than when you're single."

. . . .

"I have no appetite when it comes to sex."

Age: 28
Identifies as: Female
Has sex with: Men

How many people have you had sex with recently?
"Maybe 10."

How often do you have sex?
"Maybe 3 to 5 times a month."

How do you meet the people you are sleeping with?
"I meet people I have sex with in social spaces. Now I am in a committed relationship."

Describe your sex life.
"I would describe it as okay, I do not have an appetite when it comes to sex."

The Verdict

Sex outside of relationships can take many forms. There's just-dating-around sex, I-just-got-out-of-a-relationship sex, we-met-right-before-last-call sex, and so on. As women, we're often brought up on sexuality-shaming rhetoric: sex is tacitly accepted, but usually within the context of a relationship. But, what about all the times we're not in relationships? What then? We've all heard, "Why would a man buy the cow when you're giving him the milk for free?", and it's a tired, South African adage.

Sex is sex in any way. It's all about how you define and view it, and it boils down to how you would like to live your life. But remember, with better awareness you can make better choices, and with better choices comes better results. What single people need to understand is that sex in actual fact is a union between the body, soul, and mind of two individuals. Everyone has the right to choose and not be ridiculed for their choices but with free will comes great responsibility and huge consequences. The question we as singles should ask ourselves before diving into sex is whether we are ready to face the challenges that come ahead. It's all about researching the consequences and benefits of having sex and weighing them against each other. Do not do things ignorantly, without thought, because with ignorance the price to pay is high.

Some interesting books to read as a single person include:

1. *I Almost Forgot About You* by Terry McMillan
2. *How To Find And Choose The Right Life Partner* by Dr. Joseph Kansema

The Diary of the Married

These are very interesting interviews where we get into the thoughts and minds of married people. As you read, note that the challenges faced by married people are very similar yet different. Look at the differences between the male and female experiences. Be open-minded and truthful with yourself; don't be biased but consider the fact that these are other people's real-life stories. Begin to ask yourself, "What is *my* sex story"?

. . . .

"We are happy with our sex life."

Age: 28
Identifies as: Female

How long have you been married?
"1 year now."

How often do you have sex?
"3-4 times a week, sometimes more."

Describe your sex life.
"Healthy. I feel my husband is always in sex mode when I am not. It's generally a good idea to always have sex in the abstract but in reality, it's something else. But we are happy with our sex life in general."

"I wish we could have more sex in a week."

Age: 42
Identifies as: Male

How long have you been married?
"About 2 and a half years now."

How often do you have sex?
"2-3 times a week."

Describe your sex life.
"Amazing. My wife has all these new tricks she just pulls up from her sleeve like a genie in a bottle. I wish we could have more sex in a week, but what can I say? I have to respect that she might not always be ready, so what I do to make up for that is to masturbate. She does not like it, so I kind of have to hide the fact that I'm doing it."

"It becomes better with time."

Age: 73
Identifies as: Female

How long have you been married?
"45 years."

How often do you have sex?
"Whenever we can." *Giggles*

Describe your sex life.
"It got better with time. We understand each other and that's all that matters."

....

"I still have a fear the feeling might fade away with time."

Age: 38
Identifies as: Male

How long have you been married?
"1 year."

How often do you have sex?
"3- 4 times, and more on the weekends."

Describe your sex life.
"Very passionate and deeply fulfilling, playful with different positions. My wife is not always ready. The biggest improvement would be if I knew how to give her more pleasure and understand her body better. The best part is falling asleep together after sex, on top of or next to each other. I still have a fear that with time this feeling might fade away."

"Our sex life is questionable."

Age: 40
Identifies as: Male

How long have you been married?
"15 Years."

How often do you have sex?
"Once a month if I am lucky."

Describe your sex life.
"Questionable. I love my wife but to be honest though, I might have sex with her once a month if she agrees. I am not proud to admit that sometimes I buy sex to get the connection I desire from my wife."

The Verdict

Sex is the foundation of marriage, yet people do not know the ABCD's of sex. Marriage is the most rewarding thing in life but with great rewards come great responsibilities. It needs a lot to thrive and succeed; sex being integral, but not the only important aspect of it.

With that being said, Van de Velde in his book, *Ideal Marriage*, explains that there are four cornerstones of the temple of love and happiness in marriage:

1. *A right choice of marriage partner.*
2. *A good psychological attitude of the partners, both to the world in general and to each other.*
3. *A solution to the problem of parentage which meets the wishes of both partners.*
4. *A vigorous and harmonious sex life.*

Sex breeds intimacy. Orgasms release oxytocin, the feel-good bonding hormone, into your body. Sex helps you feel closer to your partner. It is the most intimate physical act you and your partner can experience. Without it, it's easy to lose sight of your connection. Relationships and a healthy sex life take constant work. You have to check in with each other and take the temperature of your relationship on a regular basis. Having sex, feeling your partner on top of you, and the scent of his or her skin brings you back into that loving mindset. Don't skip out on it just because you're tired from work and would rather watch television. Having maintenance sex will remind both of you what you mean to each other. Always take an opportunity to work sex into your schedule. The more you have it, the happier you can be in the relationship.

There are a lot of challenges and obstacles in marriage, but also great benefits that, without it, the lens of humanity could be distorted or fragile. If you come from a home of married parents you know this - not to say those born in singleness and not in a marriage covenant are less than others - but honestly speaking we all know it makes a difference. Van de Velde states:

"Marriage is the permanent form of monogamous erotic relationships. As such, marriage represents a distinct advance ethically; it is also evolutionary in so far as it gives the fullest opportunity for the primitive urges, which are initially purely self-regarding and self-centred, to extend themselves in action and consciousness towards altruistic objects; that is, the preservation and welfare of other persons. From this point of view, lovers who celebrate their marriage ceremony are participating in a sacred covenant, and not by any means only in the ecclesiastical sense of sacredness."

If you think about it, marriage is the only place you promise one another the highest, the loveliest, and the hardest task that man or woman can undertake. Namely, to control the current of their erotic emotions and direct it always toward each other and no one else! And throughout long years, not once, but "unto seventy times seven", to give each other that supreme joy which is the best gift that human beings can share.

This love which unfolds through marriage can permanently bless both partners in so many ways than one. But, how often do the fairest feelings fade? How often do we hear of divorce or couples confessing that they do not love each other anymore? The most earnest intentions subside. Scriptures normally reference it as this: "The spirit is willing, but the flesh is weak"[36]. However, at times even the most sincere of spirits do not remain "willing" for long.

Van de Velde discusses and explores something interesting when he states that there can be a long list of dangers, difficulties, and disasters that can cause this, such as incompatibility as times go on; differing grades of evolution; and a reaction to outdated manifestations. However, their results can only be appreciated by those who themselves experience their grief, horror, and humiliation. For the fundamental difficulty is this: that as soon as sexual attraction is extinguished, sexual repulsion and enmity manifest themselves. For there is such a thing as enmity and repulsion between the sexes: at least, among human beings.

---

36   Matthew 26:41

So the moral of the story? Sex in marriage involves great effort, patience, and selflessness from both parties to thrive and can have a satisfying, rich reward both emotionally and physically.[37]

Don't be fooled into thinking that all married people have great sex lives at the same time. Equally, don't be surprised or oblivious to the fact that some marriages have a fulfilling and great sex life. There is no life manual to this; all we need is to be open enough to talk. Communication is key. Knowledge is the door to the gates of heaven because from knowledge comes understanding, and once understanding is applied you get wisdom, which will change your relationship and sex life dramatically. Work on your marriage, talk about sex, and how to pleasure each other; read books together on such issues. Here are some recommendations:

Mating in Captivity by Esther Perel

Bonus (YOUTUBE): *Mating In Captivity - Reconciling Intimacy and Sexuality* by Esther Perel

The Meaning Of Marriage by Timothy Keller

---

37   Van de Velde (n.d.)

Why Most Wives Are Crazy And Most Husbands Are Stupid by Dr. Joseph Kansema

The Sex-Starved Marriage by Michele Weiner Davis

The Diary of the Celibate

Here we take a peak into the minds of the celibate, and their reasons behind the decision to abstain from having sex. As you read, please note that there are various reasons for celibacy and one is not more important than the other. It's interesting to see that in celibacy, whether it be for religious or personal reasons, most people are ultimately looking for the same thing: a stable, committed relationship. And those who are not looking for this are probably young and confused, or are eunuchs.

"It's for religious purposes."

Age: Undisclosed
Identifies as: Undisclosed

Why did you choose this route?
"For religious purposes."

How do you feel about it thus far?
"I'm not sure."

"Sex is a dirty exercise."

Age: 39
Identifies as: Female

Why did you choose this route?
"I think sex is a dirty exercise."

How do you feel about it thus far?
"No comment."

"I don't want to sleep with different men."

Age: 30
Identifies as: Female

Why did you choose this route?
"I don't like the idea of sleeping with different men."

How do you feel about it thus far?
"Good. It's been 3 years now."

"I want a loving connection with one man – my husband."

Age: 32
Identifies as: Female

Why did you choose this route?
"I want God to give me a husband."

How do you feel about it thus far?
"I'm okay. I have needs still but for this purpose, I am willing to sacrifice for a good intimate, loving connection with one man that is mine alone."

....

"I'm keeping a covenant."

Age: 25
Identifies as: Male

Why did you choose this route?
"Covenant keeping."

How do you feel about it thus far?
"I'm okay. People think I'm gay but it depends on purpose, you know?"

....

"I'm not ready."

Age: 23
Identifies as: Female

Why did you choose this route?
"I'm not ready."

How do you feel about it thus far?
"Confused. I wish someone could explain this to me: as to what to expect, how it will be, and if I should even have sex."

"I cannot just keep opening up."

Age: 40
Identifies as: Female

Why did you choose this route?
"I'm over it really."

How do you feel about it thus far?
"I need a serious man in my life. I cannot just keep opening up - I'm too old for that."

Chapter 7:
THE POWER OF SEX

In this chapter, we look at the power of sex through the lens of a young man who found himself deeply entangled in it.

True Story: Shadows

When I was in my twenties, I suffered from ED - erectile dysfunction. This means that I had a difficult time getting and keeping an erection, or having an orgasm during intercourse. I never thought of this as something that a young man like me would have a challenge with. I was really ashamed so I kept it a secret for almost a decade, yet little did I know that I was not the only guy under the age of 30 suffering from a globally known phenomenon.

At the end of 2014, I finally got the courage to confront it so I went to the urologist. He had a look at me and did not find a physical cause for the ED so he suggested that it might probably be performance anxiety. He then subscribed me with Levitra, which is an erection drug similar to Viagra. I gave it a try and it worked. I got an erection but I was unable to keep it up for long and could not orgasm. The worst part was that I had constant headaches thinking about the next pill I had to pop to have sex; it was just painful and not the ideal solution that I wanted to live with. So it led me to research the psychological aspects of sexuality. I found out that the brain is the most important sex organ. What I found quite interesting was the insights into how pornography can influence the brain.

Growing up in a small family that had strong Catholic values, my sexuality was limited. At the time when I hit puberty, the internet became the perfect tool to explore my sexuality. So when I tried having sex for the first time I had already had the full-blown experience of hardcore porn. It was an addiction. I would wake up and automatically entangle myself in it, more than 5-6 times a day. During the sexual revolution of the 20th century, masturbation and pornography had been freed of their moral constraints, so we were taught that masturbating and watching hardcore porn did not cause any harm.

Honestly speaking, the 20th century sexual revolution was necessary and important especially because it somehow liberated sexuality, but this belief *was very far-fetched. I witnessed countless experiences online that proved that pornography has a negative effect on the brain. Your brain becomes rewired especially if you are not fully developed. Consuming pornography online is very different from browsing a playboy magazine; the magazine has a limited amount of still images. So a fifteen-year-old today can have more virtual sex partners than his ancestors could have in a lifetime. This experience leads to hyper-stimulation of the brain, meaning more dopamine is released. But this effect then leads to desensitisation, meaning that at one point in your life when you do have a chance to encounter a real human body, reality might seem dull to what the internet has to offer therefore causing the brain to release less dopamine. It causes weaker and shorter arousal, which then leads to porn-induced erectile dysfunction[38].*

Once I found this out it felt like a triumph because I knew what was going on with me. The best part was knowing that this was reversible. Apparently, all I had to do was to stop masturbating and watching porn for a total of 120 days. This process is called rebooting. It's a process where the brain is given a chance to cure itself. Once I started the process of curing myself of ED, I decided that I wanted to make up for the years I had lost. So I made it a point to become a sex guru. I

---

38   Brito, J. (2018)

came up with a list of characteristics that I thought a guru in sex should possess. On the list were strength; stamina to have sex all night long; high levels of testosterone which results in strong libido; the ability to have multiple orgasms; rock hard erections for as long as I want; and lots of experience with different people knowing and having perfected all the sexual techniques there are.

That was my goal so I made a plan and I started my journey to becoming the guru of sex. I joined a gym and started to exercise regularly for strength and stamina. I did Kegel exercises which trained the BC muscles and would apparently result in stronger elections. I researched how to boost my testosterone levels and had regular checks with my physician. I hunted down and tried to implement every possible technique I could find to become the sex expert and transform myself into that vision I had created of myself as a Sex Guru. After a couple of weeks when I felt ready to test my progress, I noticed that despite the time and effort, I did not make much progress. When it was time to put on a condom I still experienced erectile dysfunction, and I still didn't have an orgasm during intercourse which made me angry and disappointed. Then it dawned on me that the Sex Guru project had one big flaw: the Greek philosopher Plato helped me grasp the concept behind that:

Plato Cave[39]

Imagine prisoners who have been chained deep in a cave since birth. Not only are their arms and legs chained, but their heads also, to the effect that they may only look in one direction and that is towards a wall.

Behind the prisoners is a large fire, and between the prisoners and the fire is a raised wall along which various puppets are moved back and forth. These puppets take many shapes and forms and when they are moved they create shadows on the wall in front of the prisoners. Behind the cave is a well-used road along which many people pass by while they are walking and talking, thus making noises that the prisoners think are being made by the shadows.

---

39 Image Accessed: https://faculty.washington.edu/smcohen/ 320/ cave.htm

Now replace the cave with a room, the wall with a screen, and the shadows with photographic imagery.

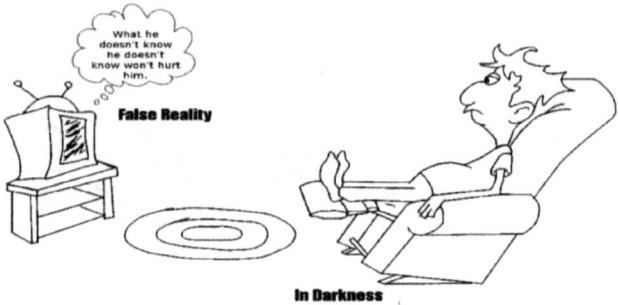

The Man Cave by Mitch Francis [40]

And that was the problem. My experience of a sexual reality was the shadows for most of my life, so I tried to imitate the shadows which are nothing but a distorted and abstracted version of reality. Pornography has the ability to limit sexuality to a passive and voyeuristic perspective whereas reality is active and immersive; it has a dimension of interpersonal connection which adds a dimension of meaning. Pornography limits sexuality to mainly the visual sense whereas the reality of sexuality is a multi-sensory experience with touch being the most important one. In the time of searching and trying to find a solution to my problem, I discovered the ultimate

---

40   Image Accessed: https://thereitis.org/the-man-cave_by_mitch -francis/

being - "God". Then I realised the answer was in front of me; God is the ultimate consciousness which in Plato's allegory is represented through the fire or sun outside.

My Sex Guru project changed and became a journey of leaving the cave, and becoming conscious of the reality of human sexuality. This was easier said than done. There were voices that whispered in my ear, "Stay in the cave, it's tranquil and secure in here". I had to fight for my happiness and break the cycle, so I made steps toward

s the exit of the cave with the help and support of my psychologist, family members, and people who had the same type of experiences. I noticed that my erectile dysfunction gradually decreased. I got married to a wonderfully beautiful goddess who helped me redefine my definition of a Sex Guru. I now define a Sex Guru as a person that constantly creates multi-sensory and meaningful sexual experiences. I learnt along the journey that sex is not just for simple reasons such as reproduction or satisfying one's personal or biological needs. I see it as an art form, a way of self-expression, and physical and emotional healing which leads to a gateway of transdermal experiences that transcend our body and mind.

Before we can get to this magical place of sexual transcendence, we first have to destroy the shackles around our minds. I really believe that the shackles represent the two most dangerous phycotoxins which are guilt and shame. We have to stop defining sex as dirty and nasty. We have to open up and make ourselves vulnerable in order to have those necessary conversations which we desperately need.

— T. King[*41]

Unlocking Sexual Wellbeing

Do you believe that you can have total control and power when it comes to sex?. Emily Nagoski in her book, **Come As You Are**, explains the Dual Control Model very profoundly. The Dual Control Model is a mechanism in the body that controls the sexual responses. This model was first suggested by researchers Bancroft and Janssen in the late 1990s:

"The first factor is the sexual excitement system or SES. This consists of everything that turns a person on. Anything that gets you sexually excited activates the SES; these things are known as accelerators. Seeing

---

41 * Name has been changed to protect the identity of the individual.

someone sexy, either in person or on a screen? A certain smell, the way your partner touches you, a sexy song, wearing lingerie, or reading erotica? All these activate the SES like pushing your foot down on the accelerator in your car."[42]

The sexual accelerator notices everything sexually relevant in the environment, from what you see, hear, smell, touch, taste, or imagine. This then sends a signal to the brain that says, "Turn!", which functions at a low level including right now. Just the fact that you are reading this book could be sexually relevant.

The second factor that works parallel to the SES is *"[t]he sexual inhibition system or SIS. The SIS is the opposite of the SES. Things that activate this system turn you off, and they're known as brakes. Brakes can be pretty obvious. Stress is a big one, so is feeling disconnected from your partner and having a poor self-image. Childhood trauma and abuse, depression, and even certain medications can act as brakes, and you might not suspect it."*[43]

Your brake notices all the good reasons not to be turned on. This also includes everything you

---

42   Gold, C. (2020)

43   Gold, C. (2020)

see, hear, smell, taste, touch, or imagine, which your brain codes as a potential threat. This then sends a signal that says, "Turn off!" Emily Nagoski puts it this way: *"The process of becoming aroused is the dual process of turning on the ons and turning off the offs."* You might wonder why sexual brakes exist at all, but there's a good reason: they prevent us from having sex that might be risky or reacting to inappropriate stimuli. Otherwise, the SES can run rampant. Usually when there is not enough stimulation to the gas pedal or there is too much stimulation to the brake that's when people struggle with sexual wellbeing. A few more common reasons for hitting the brakes include, but are not limited to:

1) Worrying about unwanted pregnancies.
2) Worrying about your children walking in while you are getting it on.
3) Being unsure of whether your partner loves your sexy body.
4) Lacking confidence in your body.
5) Spending the first decades of your life in a culture that defines sex as dangerous, disgusting, and dirty.
6) Having been sexually molested or hurt by a stranger or even someone you know.

7) Frustration with your partner and the inability to forgive them for past mistakes.

8) There is no hunt and chase anymore.

The thrill of single sex mostly comes out of the good feeling of hunting and chasing. Steve Harvey often says, *"Men are hunters. What we enjoy is the chase of the hunt"*. A lion enjoys hunting, and that is what they must do. But often in relationships, we get too comfortable and complacent. He mentions in one of his videos:

"Men are aesthetic, we're just aesthetic creatures. I love it when my wife gets jazzed up. Now if I come home 15 nights in a row, which I do often come home very late, and she is already in her little favourite boring grey sweat outfit and that's all I'm seeing for 15 days.........(awkward silence). You know I say something to my wife, "Babe we need to get up early in the morning, have breakfast together. Put on that sexy dress and do something". She ain't got no problem. She says, "Okay baby, what you want to do?" Because every now and then I want to see who I asked to marry me. I don't want to come here busting my ass and I don't get to see this person no more. No no! What the F### happened to whom I married? What am I out here working for? I'm busting my ass, she is the same person but still, you can be cute for you - that is cool.

But your man also need you to be cute for him. But you have something you require from your man too and you want it from him whether he feel like it or not. You do not have to like what I am telling you about us, it will not change us. We are who we are and if you understand that you can get what you want. I was talking to a buddy of mine who met a girl recently. I said, "How did it go buddy?" That girl was fly. He said, "Man as soon as we got home she took her make-up off." I said, "What happened?" He said, "It screwed me up." He said, "Dawg, she got to wait till I got feelings for her first. It was a total turn-off". [44]

So in a long-term relationship, women should remain chasable - sexy, attractive, gorgeous. If you were watching your weight before, watch it even more now. Men must still hunt their partners as well; it's a two-way street to *"turn on the ons and turn off the offs"*.

Power in Sex Lies With Me

Power in sex comes in taking control of your life as a whole. If you are unhappy about yourself it will eventually spill into everything else. Single people can attest to the fact that having sex during

---

44

single days when you feel young and attractive can feel very powerful. The question is: does it last? The married can also attest that having sex in a new marriage can be very powerful and fulfilling but the same question applies: does it last? This means that the problem is not sex, the problem is the people behind the act of sex. How do you feel about yourself?

Single and married people should often do self-introspection. Ask yourself these questions as a single person:

– How do I feel about my situation right now?
– Am I happy with myself as a single person?
– How does sex really feel to me emotionally?
– Can I have better sex?

As a married person you can ask yourself this set of questions:

– Am I satisfied with myself?
– Is my partner satisfied with me and if not how can I serve him or her?
– Am I just focusing on the satisfaction and comfortability of others and not of me?

[45]Let us look at a neuroscience experiment conducted on mice by a group of scientists in the Netherlands.Imagine that you are a mouse or a lab rat and the researchers have inserted a probe in your emotional brain (the front cortex of the brain which forms part of the limbic system called the amygdala and accesses the emotional value of stimuli). The researchers then assure you that it is a very painless procedure and make you feel comfortable.

They put you in a three-chambered box. You start in box number one which is the ordinary lab environment; there is a little bit of noise, the lights are on but it's okay. The researchers have explained the process to you, you are comfortable and good to go. So when the researchers zap your emotional brain you get curious: "Ooooooo… What is that?" You move your forepaws and body to the front so as to see what really just happened. Through this action, you move towards-curious-behaviour. Then in this same first box, they suddenly zap you at the back of your emotional brain which makes you jump, "What the hell is that?" You're now kicking up dust in the face of the researchers. These are stress

45   Vera Brinks*, Maaike van der Mark, Ronald de Kloet and Melly Oitzl: Division of Medical Pharmacology, LACDR/LUMC, Leiden University, The Netherlands

avoidance responses, moving you away instead of moving you towards.

Then you step into box number 2. Now, this box is the most peaceful, calm state that you can imagine being in. It's your favourite spot and has the best ambiance of soft light; you just feel relaxed collected and free. Then they zap the front of your brain again. You move your forepaws to the front with curiosity: "Oooh what is that?" Then the researchers zap the back of the emotional brain, and what do you do? You approach it with the same curiosity, "Oooh what's that?" When you are in a calm state of mind you interpret almost any sensation as something that should be approached with curiosity. Even stimulation that in a different context would be seen as a potential threat, will arouse your interest.

Now we move to box number 3. The lights are on really bright, they are playing music at differing loud volumes, and you can't even hear yourself. It feels like you are in the worst nightclub on the planet and then they zap your emotional brain. What do you think happens? You guessed it, you burst into anger. Your forepaws start kicking and scratching: "What the hell?" This means that when you are in a threatened state of mind, your brain will interpret almost anything as something to be avoided, a potential threat. If it is something you should ideally approach, you will still back away from it.

Now let's look at a real-life example like tickling. If you were feeling sexy and your special someone tickled you, you would become excited and it would probably lead to sex. But if the exact same person tickled you when you were not in such a good state of mind, what would you do? So you see, it's exactly the same contact but your brain interprets it in a different way. Turning on the ons and turning off the offs is not as simple as creating an environment or a context that allows your brain to interpret the world as a pleasurable, safe, and sexy place. For most people that context is low stress, high affection, and high trust. Getting to this state of mind is not easy; you have to work hard at unlocking the power of your sexual wellbeing. Where do we find this power? It is certainly not what we expect it to be. You find it in CONFIDENCE and JOY!

CONFIDENCE comes from knowing what is true. Knowing what is true about your body and your sexuality. Knowing that you have a brake and an accelerator, and that they are sensitive to context. It's all about knowing and having information from various sources even if it's not what you were taught to expect to be true.

JOY is loving what is true; loving your brakes as much as you love your accelerator. Loving the fact that they are sensitive to context even if it's not what you were taught to expect it to be or to be true.

How do you receive this power? When you look in the mirror, what do you see? YOU. There is no secret ingredient to sexual wellbeing, but there is YOU. You need to look internally and work on yourself the best way you can to find joy and confidence in all areas of life. Here are a few examples of how that can be done:

- Loving yourself more.
- Understanding yourself better.
- Listening to your body - exercising and eating healthy.
- Reading.
- Smiling more.
- Being more playful in relationships.
- Finding a new hobby, dancing.
- Laughing at yourself for mistakes you make.

Have you ever found it interesting why it is that during the safety briefing on a flight, they ask you to put your mask on first before you help others out? The main reason for this is because if you are suffocating and are out of air, you will not be able to save another person no matter how hard you try. You and the person you are trying to save in the worst-case scenario will most likely die. John C Maxwell in his book, *The 15 Invaluable Laws Of Growth*, asserted it this way: if you take care of you for me, I will take care of me for you.[46]

Remember, it's not a case of finding a secret ingredient. This is about day-to-day progress but for us to progress and find the power of sexual wellbeing, we as individuals need to learn new habits, then value and enjoy the process.[47]

---

46   Maxwell, J.C. (2012)
47   Nagoski online (2016)

Chapter 8:
THE PURPOSE OF SEX

What is the purpose of sex? In this chapter, we look at purpose through various stories of individuals who were kind enough to dig deep into themselves and answer the question, "What is your motive for having sex?" As you read through, ask yourself the same question.

Sex defined wholistically has five spheres: physical, emotional, social, relational, and spiritual. How do you access your sexual wholeness when you consider each of these areas? Is one area limited? Does another command all your energy? This honest self-assessment is the first step in presenting yourself with thoughts you have considered deeply so you appreciate the many interconnected and essential parts of sex. If you find that for yourself one or two of the spheres are all that sex has been for you, you are not alone. Many of us experience sex this way but this does not do justice to its potential power and value. A lack of appreciation and balance in our approach to sex may destroy the fibers that find the expression of sex in intimacy and love.

We may choose to approach sex by compartmentalizing it rather than appreciating its whole reality because we can (and often do) learn about sex in physical terms alone. We learn about it either as a form of pleasure or in its biological role for procreation, disconnected from the other spheres. Ironically, when religious authorities insist that the purpose of sex is procreation alone, they further fragment the character of sexuality. By implying that pleasure in sex is only physical or bad, and with only a spiritual purpose, we may overemphasize the spiritual sphere. While such positions are intended to preserve the sanctity of sex, they can actually create the opposite effect, losing the balance between body and spirit, and blurring the importance of healthy emotions and relationships - all equally important to sexual fulfilment.

It is very important to talk about and view sex wholistically because it affects the body, mind, and soul. If we put on a different lens and view sex as a wholistic fulfilment in life we are able to understand the connection between sex, intimacy, and love. Society does not look at sex wholistically; it takes different parts as and how it suits the moment but as an individual, knowing the difference makes the difference.

What is your motive for sex?

Psychologists have divided motives for sex into 3 types: biological, social, and personal. The biological motive is essential for the survival of all organisms which is derived out of a natural need e.g. hunger, thirst, sleep, avoidance for pain, mental drive, sex, etc. Then there are social needs which are achievement, power, curiosity, gregariousness (which simply means a need for affiliation), etc. Finally, we have personal needs like the force of habit, levels of aspiration, goals of life, attitudes, and interests. When it comes to sex, which of the 3 would best capture the motive for sex? As you ponder on this, below is a survey done with various people across the globe on what their motives are for sex.

Age: 39
Gender: Female
Status: Married
Motive: Enjoyment for both partners. Bond is formed during sex.

Age: 28
Gender: Female
Status: Single
Motive: Self-discovery; shared intimacy; an act of reciprocated service, commitment, love, and procreation.

Age: 40
Gender: Male
Status: Married
Motive: I think it has a lot of purpose, but the three main reasons for me are: 1) Reproduction; 2) Connecting with my spouse; 3) Health (Endorphins).

Age: 23
Gender: Male
Status: Single
Motive: At the stage of life where I am now, it's all about pleasure.

Age: 29
Gender: Female
Status: Single
Motive: Connection and enjoyment.

Age: 39
Gender: Male
Status: Single
Motive: Pleasure and exploring each other's sexual desires as a form of knowing each other more and also knowing yourself in the process.

Age: 30
Gender: Female
Status: Single
Motive: Connection with partner.

Age: 25
Gender: Female
Status: Single
Motive: Enjoyment, connection, and getting to know someone in terms of compatibility.

Age: 25
Gender: Female
Staus: Single
Motive: Connection with partner.

Age: 32
Gender: Female
Status: Married
Motive: To get closer; intimacy.

Age: 28
Gender: Male
Status: Married
Motive: For pleasure.

Age: 36
Gender: Male
Status: Single
Motive: Scratching the itch and quenching the thirst.

Age: 30
Gender: Female
Status: Single
Motive: Connection with partner.

Age: 36
Gender: Female
Status: Single
Motive: Intimacy and connection with partner.

Age: 39
Gender: Male
Status: Single
Motive: Fun and entertainment.

Age: 30
Gender: Female
Status: Married
Motive: To connect and for ultimate intimacy.

Age: 28
Gender: Male
Status: Single
Motive: For the excitement.

Age: 28
Gender: Male
Status: Married
Motive: For pleasure.

Age: 39
Gender: Female
Status: Single
Motive: Not sexually active but I say it's for procreation.

Age: 30
Gender: Female
Status: Single
Motive: Connection and to satisfy needs.

Age: 29
Gender: Female
Status: Single
Motive: To bring two people together both physically and spiritually. To get pleasure from someone and to also give them pleasure.

Age: 30
Gender: Male
Status: Married
Motive: For pleasure and strengthing the bond.

Age: 38
Gender: Female
Status: Married (5 years)
Motive: As a consensual act in a relationship or marriage, sex creates intimacy in a moment that fosters your relationship. It is a physical expression of emotional connection.

Age: 30
Gender: Female
Status: Married
Motive: It's a love language, for bonding, passion, and procreation.

Age: 35
Gender: Male
Status: Married
Motive: Fun, fun, and enjoyment.

More often than not the source of a problem can be traced to its particular motivation. When having problems with sex it's very relevant to ask oneself, "What is my motivation?"

If we look at the above motives closely we realise that there is a difference between the sexes. Generally, men are body-centred, meaning they seek sex because of how it makes their bodies feel. Women, although they also derive pleasure from sex, are mostly person-centred, meaning they are generally interested in the emotions, connection, and the relationship enhancement that sex offers.

As individuals, we all have different views of sex that have been inherently, socially, and factually formed in our minds due to our history, culture, and experiences, that may lead us to be biased and not fully grasp that the ultimate purpose of sex is to get wholistic fulfilment. And if we do not understand the words 'wholistic fulfilment', we only understand sex on a factual basis looking at sex as the ultimate joy that oozes from your skin and gives you a glow after the act of thrusting in and out, or of being thrusted. Which in actual truth, is only scratching the surface. To derive the wholistic fulfilment from sex we desire we have to be conscious about our unconsciousness. Simply put, be happy with oneself and love yourself enough to gain under-standing so that sex does not become a factual thing to fill a void in the heart, which might feel good in the moment, but after the effect and act may still feel empty, dull, and daunting to the soul.

Chapter 9:
THE PRODUCT OF SEX

Why do you sleep at night? This is a seemingly simple question, but in actual fact it is a most difficult question to answer. Many seemingly simple questions are, on close inspection, not at all easy to answer. One of these - perhaps the most interesting - is, "Why do we have sex?" Well, based on the known functions of sex no one can dispute that our continued existence as species depends on it; children are the product of sex. The story about children falling from a tree no doubt is a terrible joke. What is really surprising is that we have conjectures on procreation and sex because long after we, the human species, have had children we still continue to engage in sex. Why? At most, if we are lucky it may be because our sex lives might be better as there are no worries about children walking in on us, or because we have no worries of unwanted pregnancies. Who knows?

Today, most of the sex that is happening out there is not for procreation. In fact, people get upset when they find out that their joyful acrobatics have resulted in unwanted pregnancies. We find that the interest in sex is inversely related to the interest in producing offspring. Moreover, many sexual behaviors we commonly engage in, even in the fertile years, are not related to reproduction at all. If sex is for reproduction, how is the mechanism of sexual pleasure organized regarding anal or oral sex? And why are you holding hands with your boyfriend? Children do not come of it. Besides, you also hold hands with your three-year-old niece. What's going on here? And what is reproductive about someone pulling your hair? In fact, why does the business of genital reproductive pleasure spread to all kinds of remote areas not related to reproduction, such as shoulders (very sexy in the nineteenth century), the neck (sexual attraction in Japanese culture), or breasts (contemporary American obsession), and the hips and bums (African obsession)? And if men have a biological urge to find a good mother for their offspring, why do they routinely differentiate between a 'sexy' woman and a 'motherly' one, and prefer the former to the latter?

Okay, let's step aside from the obvious biological factors. Sex feels good - most of us can agree with that. It's fun and pleasurable. However, that argument, even though relevant, is also unsatisfactory because in essence sexual pleasure is just a mirror effect of the real reason for sexual intimacy. If you really think about it, if it's the pleasure you want, you can easily get it through self-stimulation or masturbation. So the question is, why are you having sex with another person and calling it pleasurable? And why is it when you masturbate you fantasise about him or her? This could possibly mean that outside of that, the deep experience of sexual pleasure depends somehow on the presence - and conduct - of others.

A blunt illustration of this principle can be found in prostitution. On its face, prostitution is a cold business - the epitome of (mostly male) selfish pleasure-seeking. The customer buys physical sexual release for money. Plain and simple. But the customer could give himself an orgasm for free. So why pay? And why is the customer's enjoyment increased if the prostitute produces the sounds of enjoyment and sexual arousal? If the client's motivation is selfish sexual release - the satisfaction of a biological urge - why does it matter to him if the prostitute is aroused? What excites him about the thought that she is enjoying herself? Fundamental social interpersonal dynamics are apparently present even here, inside the most alienated transaction. Beyond this factor, if we look at it in reality sex is not automatically enjoyable. Remember your first sexual experience? Was it fun?

To help us answer these questions, let's look at a survey found online that was conducted on several individuals who were kind enough to share their first sexual experience.

My First Sexual Experience: Anonymous Testimonies [48]

Age then: 18
Age now: 23
"It was extremely painful and highly regretful. I did it with a boy during my school's senior week. He had a girlfriend and was sleeping with one of my friends, but also had sex with me that weekend. I was very drunk, and I hated every single second of it. I wish it never happened like that, but I guess it's a good bar story."

48   Barcella, L. (2018)8

Age then: 16
Age now: 33
"I was dating a Jehovah's Witness drug dealer who would get high and then get sad that I was going to hell because I was Catholic. But, I wanted to have sex so bad that I didn't care. We got drunk and climbed onto his waterbed. It was broken, so he'd laid a twin mattress over it. I had to try very hard not to get seasick while he jammed a rather insanely large penis into my vaginal area. When it was done, he cried again because I was going to hell."

Age then: 17
Age now: 30
"I was at this hot surfer boy's studio apartment in Boston. He was 23 — I'd met him on a trip to Bermuda during my senior year in high school. I'd waited so long. I felt like I was in love with him. After it was over, I kept waiting for him to say something deep and meaningful, like, you know, 'I love you.' Instead, he looked over and said, 'Damn girl, your shit's the bomb.'"

Age then: 18
Age now: 39

"In [my friend's] basement after school, we were making out, and then...all of a sudden, he was inside me. I didn't say no, and it wasn't painful... But, I felt a lot of shame afterward that I had...just 'let [this guy] do it' on, like, our third date.

"About a week later, he broke up with me, [saying] we were better as friends. I didn't sleep with anyone [again] for three years.

"It wasn't until recently, when I started to really understand consent and emotional manipulation, that I felt safe saying that I was raped."

Age then: 20
Age now: 34

"We went back to his place, drank some beers by his pool, and boned on the couch. I don't remember it feeling great, but I don't remember it being awful. It sort of felt like nothing."

Age then: 17
Age now: 39
"We did not 'date.' [The guy I liked] simply came over one night when my parents were attending family therapy, [which] was a mandatory part of the outpatient rehab I was being forced to do. It wasn't good sex. It wasn't painful, but it wasn't enjoyable. I felt relief that I was no longer a virgin, but I do regret becoming involved with that boy because he turned out to be a complete asshole. I did get very attached to him after the sex, but I don't know if it was because it was my first time or just [because I was] so hungry for attention."

Age then: 20
Age now: 50
When my boyfriend of eight months and I were ready to be intimate for the first time, he [took me to] a sleazy motel, complete with red lights and beer cans discarded in the parking lot. His first words afterward? 'We shouldn't have done this.'"

Age then: 20
Age now: 31
"It was very sleazy and dirty, the guy was a total nutcase. I wish it had been someone else."

Age then: 18
Age now: 44
"He was an honest loser, I was young and naïve. If I could go back to my younger self I would have kept my virginity till married and avoided a whole lot of problems."

Of course, these are just a fraction of different experiences and some are better or worse than others. *"Even if we focus on the genitals, most of the sexual organs are very sensitive to touch - for better or worse. If someone touches your genitals clumsily, or when you're not ready or do not want to be touched, the contact will be painful, offensive, and disgusting, not exciting and pleasurable. The point is that good sex is learned; you have to work for it. It does not show up on its own. And it is not just about you alone. Sexual pleasure, it seems, is set up, operated, defined, and organized by external factors."*[49]

---

49   Shpancer, N. (2012)

"Randall Collins, the great American sociologist who's been writing on the subject for decades… argues quite persuasively that human sexuality can be fully understood only in a social context. Human beings, fundamentally, are distinctly, spectacularly social."

It's hard to imagine living in a world of isolation; being alone is one of the most devasting experiences for the human species. As human beings, purpose and meaning in this life emerge through making connections and being able to touch others through words, body, and soul. Sexual desire, or instinct, therefore, is not only for procreation and the pleasure one feels, but to connect with people to build a bridge where we can feel loved, desired, and wanted because as we all know being desired, wanted, and loved is a need; a need expressed in so many different ways in which sex plays an important role. Being connected is part of the product of sex, that is why many times people pay for sex. What are they looking for? In essence, there is no sale without a product and the product people are looking for is physical touch, being wanted, safety in the moment, comfort, and joy in the feeling - which at the end of the day points out to a product called connectivity - that can only be given by another human being.

Chapter 10:
THE SEX CONTAINER

"And do not imitate this world, but be transformed by the renovation of your minds, and you shall distinguish what is the good, acceptable and perfect will of God." [Romans 12:2, Aramaic Bible in Plain English]

Most times we as humans are not able to manage or understand the area of sex and Christianity. As mentioned in chapter 1, not even the church knows how to approach it. We fight it because we don't understand it. But in this chapter, allow yourself to dive deep, debone, and deconstruct some interesting facts that you might not have known before. I encourage you to take a deep breath and maybe get a cold glass of water for this one.

We cannot separate sex from its Creator. Society has tried to quantify sex through music, movies, advertisements, and many other artifacts that entice our minds and lure us into thinking sex was created by human strength. This in turn pushes us further away from understanding the true beauty of sex. Jesus in the scriptures explains, *"The thief comes only in order to steal, kill, and destroy. I have come in order that you might have life--life in all its fullness."* [John 10:10, Good News Translation] Most of us even right now are engaging in selective reading; we see *"The thief comes only in order to steal, kill and destroy"*. But in actual fact, if you read deeper and look at the word **only** (in this context used as an adverb) it literally enhances the meaning of the sentence specifying that the thief does not come unless there is something to kill, steal, and destroy. In this passage, the word thief refers to the enemy/bad spirits/the devil. What I found interesting is that the devil is not omnipresent, meaning he can't be everywhere at the same time. Therefore, what he does is set up structures that will keep us entangled for years on end. These structures can come in many different forms and might be as common as sex addiction, pornography, and lack of esteem, or individualised to the person based on factors such as experience, how you were taught about sex, and how you perceive yourself and the world.

To give a brief background, below are stories that encapsulate the title of this chapter from real events and face-to-face interviews.

True Story: The Sex Covenant

Before I got married, I was in prayer and I told God, "I do not want to live like this anymore. I am tired of being a softball to men who are just interested in my vagina and not interested in me as a person. I want to eventually get married to someone who will appreciate me, not just want me for sex but also want me for my character, my mind, and my presence." So I made a list of the kind of man I wanted and made a covenant with God saying, "Lord I will close my legs and control my emotions until You grant me the man I prayed for."

And behold it was opened a fountain of water for me; it was raining men left, right, and center. It was as if I had asked God to confuse me even further. I thought WTF. Mind you these were handsome men who were exactly my type. I am certain that if I had not been serious in my request I would have taken the opportunity to have sex with different men at least twice a week. I went back in prayer and I said, "God, what is the meaning of this? Are you trying to make me see that I'm making a mistake and I should live out my sex life and just be happy?"

Then it dawned on me in that instant that because I had made such a covenant the Universe and everything agreed and sealed the deal but there was part of it that did not want me to do it. The positive and negative forces were fighting each other and I had a choice; instant gratification which no-one knew where it would lead, or a beautiful predictable future that I had prayed for. I chose the latter. Of course, the men did not stop coming, but the more they all came - because I knew what I wanted and was adamant - the more I stood my ground. This went on for 2 years until I met someone who when I said, "Excuse me sir I am not having sex till I am married", he said, "Okay, I have not been having sex for a while myself because I am looking for someone with whom to spend the rest of my life." We got married, had beautiful sex and the rest is history.

—*S. Whittle*[*50]

True Story: Empty

For years, I denied that there was anything wrong. No, I was just acting like a 'real man'. You see, our

---

50 * Name has been changed to protect the identity of the individual.

society makes it so easy for guys to hide behind constructed ideals of masculinity. We're taught that it's natural for men to be 'sex-driven' and that 'boys will be boys.' For too long, this notion has allowed sexual predators to get away with heinous and misogynistic acts. But it has done something else too; it has provided a hiding place for those of us who are addicted to sex. I had thought of myself as sexually liberated, but the truth was sex had imprisoned me. It was always there, occupying my thoughts day and night. I always insisted that I simply had a high sex drive. But when I looked back on the evidence, the truth began to settle uneasily in my stomach. I almost constantly craved sexual gratification. It didn't matter how. It could be with my partner, a total stranger, or with my right hand; I always needed it. It wasn't unheard of for me to reach orgasm four or more times a day, particularly in my late teens and early twenties. The longer I went without cumming, the more irrational I'd get. We've all heard the term 'hangry' when someone becomes irritable because they're hungry. Well, I got 'sex angry' when I was horny. All I could think about was when I was going to shoot my next load; I was notorious for thinking with my penis instead of my heart.

In nearly every other facet of my life, I was responsible, mindful, and logical. But when it came to

149

sex, I couldn't control myself. It was as if at the first hint of getting some action, some foreign entity would seize control of my body, overriding my maturity and sense of personal safety. I began to see that my behavior was no different than a drug user getting desperate for their next hit. Sex hadn't just become a source of pleasure, it had become a way of showing that I was macho and I could get any woman I wanted. However, deep inside I was empty and never really enjoyed the presence of these women after I had relieved myself. I had weaponized sex to shield my pain, self-loathing, and depression. I used sex as a way to ignore my problems and feel wanted and desired. I believed it would make up for my emotional issues and lack of self-esteem.

—*Paul Majola**[51]

True Story: Lack of Self-Love

A little after I turned thirty, I stumbled upon a realisation about myself and discovered that I was a sex addict.

This truth dawned on me one cold July morning in Jozi, as I awoke in a room I had never seen before. It was dingy, poorly lit, with wallpaper peeling in

---

51 * Name has been changed to protect the identity of the individual.

virtually every corner, and a small crack across the window. The only furniture was a mattress and an innerspring in the middle of the room. The mattress had no linen on it and based on the stains, it had seen a variety of human fluids throughout its lifetime.

The rattling sound of snoring interrupted my blurry thoughts, and as I turned a man was sleeping next to me. I tried to figure out what his name was but no name came to mind. He was not the man I met at the bar, nor was he the guy I flirted with in the nightclub's dirty bathroom. I vaguely recalled being in a taxi with someone. Maybe it was this man? The used condoms discarded on the side of the bed suggested a busy evening even though I had no idea who this dude was.

I thought of my boyfriend whom I had been dating for two years and felt an emptiness inside. I quickly jumped to my phone which was on a chair next to the mattress. There was a single text: 'Where are you?!' It was him. While he knew I had an insatiable sexual appetite, it made me feel guilty and ashamed that I was doing this to him. He was an amazing person - I could not have wished for anyone different but my problem was that I was not satisfied, and more often than not I'd find myself creeping back to my old habits and physical temptation.

I tiptoed around the disgusting room, putting on my clothes, and planned to make a swift exit before my latest sexual conquest woke-up and attempted to start another round or worse... conversation. I left the apartment without looking back, no note, no phone number, and headed outside. The street was no better than the apartment, and I recognized nothing. Not the street name, no landmark, absolutely nothing. Where the hell was I?!

This wasn't the first time I had woken up unaware of where I was. I had done it plenty of times, and somewhat unconsciously it was satisfying to have casual sex then disappear. One time back in university, I went home with a random guy only to discover the next morning that I was in a completely different city almost two hours away. My one-night stander for the night was kind enough to give me the money to take a bus back home. So, here I was again, unsure of where I was or who I had been with. Why did I keep doing this to myself?

There had been moments of clarity over the years where I'd momentarily allow myself to see the truth. I vividly remember coming home after a particularly rough hookup. I had bite marks all over my body, light choke-marks around my neck, and some bruising on my legs. I looked at myself completely naked and allowed myself to truly feel how damaged I was. I broke down and sobbed to the point of throwing up. I felt an emptiness in my heart and a burning hatred in my stomach. A chorus of "you're a worthless whore" played in my head repeatedly. Yet, after an hour I pulled myself together, freshened up, and headed out to another party where I went to bed with someone new. I used sex as a defence mechanism; a way for me to bury my pain and feelings of worthlessness. You see, I didn't like myself. I had never really allowed myself the opportunity to grow into my own skin, to love the woman I had become.

— *Sonia Peterson*[*52]

True Story: Tête-à-Tête

Below is a conversation between a Pastor and someone who was kind enough to be part of this story. This is an interesting conversation which, if you read with an open mind, might assist in capturing the essence of containing sex and practicing self-discipline

Young Man: *"Yeah, that was me. When I was horny I would just call someone. I would look*

---

52 * Name has been changed to protect the identity of the individual.

down my contacts to see who would be the next
candidate. I have a separate phone where I just
keep these contacts and I scroll down when I'm
hot and bothered. They're easy to find but during
lockdown, it was especially hard. However, I
found my way around it to release myself because
hey, the pressure was too tough to handle. Even
now I still do it. I might know I'm wrong and yes
it bothers me a little bit, but I just cannot control
my urges and I feel like this God that everyone is
talking about is just making things worse for me.
He made me this way so what do you expect me to
do? On a serious note, I do not know how to stop
the feeling and if you have any advice, I'm
listening to you."

Pastor: Let's look at an interesting verse in
Corinthians. "You say, 'Food was made for the
stomach, and the stomach for food.' (This is true,
though someday God will do away with both of
them.) But you can't say that our bodies were
made for sexual immorality. They were made for
the Lord, and the Lord cares about our bodies."[53]

What Paul is saying here is that it is very true
that food was made for the stomach. If you are
hungry you have to eat right? But don't compare
eating food with satisfying your sexual desires.

---

53   1 Corinthians 6:13 [New Living Translation]

When you are horny you cannot have the same response.

Many of us have been fulfilling our sexual appetite because we feel it's natural and Paul here is saying you cannot look at your body the same way you look at food when you are hungry because that was not the main intention for it. Our bodies were made for the Lord. And the Lord cares about your body."

Young Man: *"I hear you Pastor but still how do I control this as I did not ask to be horny and God gave me this body?"*

Pastor: *"Son, when faced with natural desires we try to deal with them naturally, but the Creator is saying if you allow Me to be in the centre of the situation I can give you a better way that will allow you not to face the consequences of your own actions. You just need to give it to Me. So don't treat your body like you would treat your stomach when getting a McDonald's meal. Don't just go get what will please you for a moment because your body was not made for that."*

Young Man: *"But what is sexual immorality? I am certainly not doing anything considered to be immoral. It's such a gruesome word."*

Pastor: *"Sexual immorality comes from the Greek word 'porneia' which means the selling of something very valuable for cheap. So that is why you will find young women and men exposing the secret places of themselves for a penny, and selling off the thing that God calls so special and so pure. The Creator says that your bodies were made to give Him glory; sex is an act of worship to the Creator that is why He does not want you to 'porneia' (sell it off for cheap). It's valuable; imagine me taking my cellphone and using it as a cup holder?"*

Young Man: *"Yeah right!!! (angrily) But why did He give me all the urges and this rage?"*

Pastor: *"Because He wants you to be dependent on Him. See, don't miss the story of the Bible; the story is that His love covers all of your sins but you can't live this life without Him and His power that helps you overcome all temptations."*

So what is the moral of the story? Here is when we have to ponder and have a discussion with ourselves; we are all individuals with different backgrounds, needs, and wants. But if we let our desires lead to our decisions just as in the story above, our lives (and our bodies) can quickly spin out of control. The "sex container" is just a simple way of exercising self-control.

Biblical Anecdote

Going back to the Bible let us focus on Paul when he wrote a letter to the Corinthians. To paint a picture of what he was dealing with at the time here is a question: have you been to Las Vegas before? If you have not, you must have heard about it or seen it in movies. But the most important thing to note is that Las Vegas caters to lust; sin city at its best. You will find prostitutes at every corner and what is more flabbergasting is that in every restaurant you find a slot machine in the toilet. So you can gamble while releasing your faeces. Awesome idea, right?

If you look back at the history, Corinth was a sex-charged city where there were prostitutes in the synagogue just waiting to be picked up. Much like our world today, which caters to such behaviours and desires. That was the situation Paul was trying to deal with; these people were battling with the idea of serving God and still being in a sexually charged environment. Here, Paul was tormented by their careless indulgent attitude. We are not told what questions were submitted for Paul to answer through a letter but let's imagine the questions were something along the lines of:

How do we deal with this? And why are you not having sex man?

There are prostitutes everywhere. How do we handle our urges?

I'm single too Paul. We see you are not sexually active but do we have to be like you?

I have urges Paul. I'm married and my wife is not giving me sex. Can I just get it from somewhere else?

Paul, God made us this way. What do you want us to do when we are horny?

His reply, in my opinion, was hilarious: "Don't fool yourselves. Don't you realise that those who engage in sexual immorality will not inherit the kingdom of God?" You can imagine their thoughts, "This guy is foolish. Stupid even. And does not know what he is rambling on about. Shut up Pauly! You are a virgin. What do you know about vaginas and penis'?" Still to this day we know of people who would not mind strangling Paul for such comments.

Clearly, Paul was anti-prostitution. Paul was anti a lot of things. This is one of the reasons so many people disliked him so much. Come to think of it, this is also the reason so many love Paul so much. Today, those who dislike Paul usually dislike him because of the way his guidelines for sexual activity (and gender roles, and interactions with slaves, and castration, etcetera) have been preached as moral law. Some churches tend to avoid the topic of sex altogether, usually in response to those churches who obsess over it and preach it in ways to induce guilt and shame.

In his letter, Paul goes into a riff on sexual purity, specifically regarding intercourse with prostitutes; Paul finds sex with prostitutes problematic because sex with a prostitute typically happens without a spiritual union. Since Paul believes that the body and spirit are connected, not temporarily but eternally, what we do to and with our bodies matters. Yes, that tattoo with Chinese characters that you don't know the meaning of will still be on your ankle when you arrive at the "pearly gates of heaven".

The question here is, is Heaven the only destination? And what is the kingdom of God in context with what Paul is saying? Eckhart Tolle puts it this way: the kingdom of God is the simple profound joy of being that is there when you let go of all identifications. There are so many things people can identify themselves with but in the case of sex, you can identify yourself as not normal because you don't feel pleasured by sex. You can identify yourself as an addict. You can identify yourself with guilt and shame. You can identify yourself with past pain; as a rape victim or a victim of molestation.

It is good to have an 'I am going to heaven' mentality but that is just a small frame of the big picture. Most people think or see the kingdom of God as some mystical beautiful place in Heaven where you will have a large house with golden carpets and golden windows opening up to God. As a result, they agree to live in the world today in mediocrity. On a serious note, though, what do you think will happen once you have reached Heaven? Do you think you will have a physical body and enjoy the pleasures of sex? Or that there will be beautiful women and handsome men waiting there just to pleasure you? Is that the highest form of achievement? Why not enjoy sex and life now? Your Creator wants you to break the shackles that have been holding you back and live your best life now. Today, have amazing sex - today, now. Not tomorrow but now. But for that to happen we come back to the confidence and joy we spoke about in the previous chapter, and truth be told we cannot have an amazing life - or in this case, mindblowing sex - if we do not loosen the shackles of identification and identify with the Creator.

Paul then continues to say, *"Now for the matters you wrote about: 'It is good for a man not to have sexual relations with a woman.' But since sexual immorality is occuring, each man should have sexual relations with his own wife, and each woman with her own husband. The husband should fulfill his marital duty to his wife, and likewise the wife to her husband."*[54]

Now if you read it out of context this is what you will understand: Do not have sex because it's wrong and immoral, but in actual fact, putting it in context to the whole scripture Paul is cautioning people by saying, "You know what? It is okay if you become like me but it's really tough and if you can not control yourselves please go ahead and get married." But this also does not mean just marry anyone for the purpose of sex. We have to be sensible sometimes and think beyond the literal words of scripture and put pieces of the puzzle together with wisdom. People say the bible is complicated. It's not. In actual fact, we are the common denominator and the complicated ones.

---

54   1 Corinthians 7:1-3 [New Internation Version]

True Story: Married and Tied

My father was a Pastor and I was next in line to succeed him. I did everything I could to make him proud; I followed all the rules, even ones I did not fully grasp at the time. My mother and I had a very good relationship and I had a promising relationship with my Creator. When I turned 21 I met my first girlfriend and we dated for about 2 weeks then she got bored of my actions as a celibate man and started asking for sex. I realise now she was insecure and wanted to feel loved through sex but by then I was also insecure.

She was amazing, had all the great qualities you would want in a woman. I had never kissed a girl before so her soft lips - even just a peck - brought tears to my eyes. I was so in love but stood my ground even though my body was fighting me tooth and nail. She kept on begging me for sex, touching me, enticing me. Deep down I knew that the way she was horny all the time, meant she had a problem. I could sense that she was unfaithful, insecure, and had serious life issues but I went to my mother and said, "Sarah is asking me for sex." My mom looked at me and said, "You know exactly what to do if you want to have sex."

So a few months later we got married; my body was tingling but my heart was doubting. After the small rushed wedding, we finally had sex. Ooooh it was not what I expected nor what she expected either! I felt like a stick swimming in the River Nile, just floating. The fact that she was so adamant about sex did not alert me to the fact that she was broken and I joined myself to that brokenness. That night out of disappointment, we cancelled the honeymoon and I left for a holiday with my friends. We were married and had kids but because of her insecurities, her brokenness, and lack of commitment (she was sleeping with other men), after 5 years we divorced. To be honest, I regret the decision I made to get married just for sex; it's not worth it.

—*Jim Jones*[*55]

Consider the question or concern Paul must have been answering when he famously said, "… each man should have his own wife and each woman her own husband."[56] Paul wasn't instructing everyone to get married out of desire. No, Paul wants already-married people to not refrain from sex with one another. By saying, "each man should have his own wife," Paul means you have a choice after choosing to stick to that and indulge in your own partner... At the

---

55   * Name has been changed to protect the identity of the individual.

56   1 Corinthians 7:11

time, and in the Hellenistic culture, there was a popular notion that if one could be celibate, one could reach new spiritual heights. You will recognize that this is an attitude that is commonly felt and held.

Paul knew the beauty of celibacy but he also knew the dangers if you did not understand why you were celibate, and what it really stood for. He also knew the beauty of marriage and the dangers that come with it. If we look clearly, Paul was actually clarifying to the Corinthians so that they wouldn't fall into the trap of imagining they'd be holier than the rest by remaining or becoming celibate. Additionally, he was trying to help the Corinthians avoid the damage that adultery (prostitution, unfaithfulness, etc) often causes when spouses decide to find sex elsewhere.

In layman's terms if Paul was alive I think he would say, "Are you married? Then have sex as often as you can and be creative in the bedroom. Celibate? Research, find yourself, and have the correct motives for celibacy, to help you go through your personal journey. Remember knowledge is power. Singles, the most exhilarating thing about life is that you have the power to choose your own course, including sexually."

CONCLUSION

L et's look at the following pictures[57] to help us better understand the need for sex to be contained as we have learnt in the previous chapter.

Maybe you didn't realise the fact that sex has immense power. Maybe you didn't realise that it has to be contained. Maybe you didn't realise that when you put sex "in" something that can handle the power it becomes something that can generate life for you and others.

Hundreds of thousands of gallons of water contained produce power for an entire city because it's in the right container. But what does water look like uncontained?

---

57 Image taken from Financial Express online: https://www. financialexpress.com/opinion/damning-the-dam-should-dams-be-blamed-for-flooding-real-reasons-may-lie-elsewhere/1337842/

The picture above is a dam reservoir in India

It looks like destruction, like devastation. It looks like it can get inside parts of our lives we never thought it could get into, and even if it leaves, it leaves residue and we can be dealing with the ramifications of it for years to come.

Water uncontained can be disastrous, but the same water contained can provide light to a city and nourish human bodies.

The picture on the next page depicts the disastrous ramifications of flooding in Kenya in 2018 [58]

---

58   Images taken from Shelterbox online: https://www.shelterbox. org/where-we-work/kenya-flooding/

"Do you not know that your body is a temple of the Holy Spirit who is in you, whom you have received from God? You are not your own; you were bought at a price. Therefore glorify God with your body." [1 Corinthians 6:20-21, Berean Study Bible]

This means you are valuable; a very rare and prized possession, and maybe you did not realise this. You have a Manager - your Creator - who wants to help you manage all issues including sexual urges and all the niceties that come with it. The question is, who owns you? Does sex own you? Because what owns you, manages you.

If you have an apartment and you are renting it, the key to doing that successfully is having good ownership because if something breaks or gets damaged in the house you are not responsible because you don't own it. The owner comes in to manage that property. So if you are experiencing sexual urges, pain from the past, soul ties, suffering, or struggling and you own you, you are doomed. But if the Divine owns you He can bring management into your life. As you answer the question "Who owns you?", also know that the beauty of life is that you and I have the freedom to choose our path. Everything is definitely permissible but not everything is beneficial.

If you read this book and are this far, it would be helpful to do some self-introspection.

If you are married, what is happening in your bedroom? Are you having enough sex or is it so dry that it encourages bad behaviour from partners?

If you are single, how is your sex life? Are you truly happy with your sex life?

If you are celibate, what is the reason behind it? are you using this decision for the purposes of being holier than thou?

Remember, everything is permissible but not everything is beneficial.

EPILOGUE

If you have read this far you are a hero. All of us have freedom of choice and we are all entitled to make decisions with information that is sound and accurate. I hope that through the book I was able to inform you and grant you a deeper level of knowledge about sex. Through my pain and my scars, I was able to produce this book so that I may show you that I am not ashamed. I hope that you too will find a way to acknowledge your past, rework and reframe your future. The beautiful part of life is that we all have choices, and unlike primates, we can decide, rework, and reframe our lives and perspectives of sex and life.

The past, whether it was out of choice or an unfortunate circumstance, this too shall pass. While we are alive it is our duty to learn, gain knowledge and understanding with and from each other. To start afresh or even remain the same. But who can remain the same with new knowledge and insight?

ABOUT THE AUTHOR

Laila Benzel is a South African. She is married and currently lives and works in Germany. As a Transformative Coach, she focuses on relationships across the board; helping people flourish in their personal and work relationships is her passion.

She is also a member and a certified speaker of the John Maxwell Team. Laila lives her life as a servant leader.

A tragic experience in her childhood not only disrupted her formative years but misconstrued and tainted her view of sex as an adult and in her quest for healing, she was compelled to write this book. This book shares true stories, including her own, that explore and unmask the complexities of sex. She gives a wholesome view on the impact of sex in our lives and how we can begin to approach it in a more natural, free, and meaningful way.

SEX-Rated is a compelling non-fiction book that covers different topics from taboo, religion, and addiction. It takes you into people's bedrooms as it explores sex in marriage, sex outside of marriage, as well as celibacy. This book is based on extensive research and diverse interviews, from a 73-year-old sharing her life with a giggle, to a rather confused taxi driver, and more.

ACKNOWLEDGEMENTS

My nieces and nephews, Daisy, Carla, Thelma, Neo, Jessica, Gabriela, Danniela, Irah, Wanga, Willa, Mali, Taiyo, Neo; my cousins Mira and Nercia; and those yet to come: Words cannot express my love for you all. You are the main reason I wrote this book. Every page, every word, every chapter, every letter, and every breath is inspired by you. My prayer is that all of you find fulfilment and purpose in this lifetime and that none of you get thrown off course due to a lack of knowledge, temptations, or any type of addiction that life might offer. I pray that you learn from my experiences. I pray that you find wisdom, light, and love that will last an eternity. Watching you grow has been an immense joy to me but the greatest joy will be me leaving seeds of purity in your hearts that you will later utilise.. May my footprints be drawn in your heart through this book.

My brother, Victor: You and I have been through struggles some more similar than others but, we continue to rise. May this book be proof that struggles and experiences are what make us interesting human beings. I know deep down in my heart that the Lord is moulding a legend out of you that is to be unleashed into the world.

My Dearest Mother: I love you and I forgive you for all the mistakes you think you made when raising me. Now that I am older I understand that you are perfect in your imperfections and that you tried your best to make me the strong, successful woman I am today and for that, I thank you now and forever.

Sonia: My sister, my friend, I am grateful for your support throughout this journey. Thank you for giving me strength and courage when I needed it most.

Pastor Joseph Kansema: As a spiritual father you have inspired me with your biblical teachings, Your rawness to tackle, and the ability talk about truth in a way that enlightens and challenges is powerful. Consequently my life has changed.

Grant: Words can not express how much I am thankful for your support. This book has been an idea for almost a decade and you took the bucket and drew it out forcefully and patiently. I would not have done this without you.

To my heroic spouse: You have always held the standards high. Thank you for your patience and support that has sustained me throughout this journey.

To My Creator: Thank You for guiding me through and for helping me to turn potential into purpose. You continue to be faithful in all situations. Thank You!

BIBLIOGRAPHY

Barcella, L. (2018). *34 Women Get Real About Losing Their Virginities.* Accessed online: https://www.refinery29. com/en-us/first-time-sex-experience#slide-8

Basic Introduction to Soul Ties. Accessed online: https:// www.greatbiblestudy.com/deliverance-ministry/ basic-introduction-to-soul-ties/

Brito, J. (2018). *How can porn induce erectile dysfunction?* Accessed online: https://www.medicalnewstoday. com /articles/317117

Burleson, M.H., Trevathan, W.R., & Todd, M. (2006). *In the Mood for Love or Vice Versa? Exploring the Relations Among Sexual Activity, Physical Affection, Affect, and Stress in the Daily Lives of Mid-Aged Women.* Accessed online: https://link.springer.com/article/10.1007/ s10508-006-9071-1

Business Wire online (October, 2018): https://www. businesswire.com/news/home/20181002005775/en/ The-Global-Adult-Toys-Market-was-Worth-23.7Bn-in-2017-and-is-Projected-to-Reach-35.5Bn-by-2023---A n a l y s i s - b y - T y p e - a n d - R e g i o n - - - ResearchAndMarkets.com#:~:text=com%20%7C%20 Business%20Wire-,The%20Global%20Adult%20 T o y s % 2 0 M a r k e t % 2 0 w a s % 2 0 W o r t h % 2 0 %2423.7Bn%20in,Type%20and%20Region%20

%2D%20ResearchAndMarkets.com

Clarke, M. (n.d.). *What's Going On With Hormones And Neurotransmitters During Sex.* Accessed online: https://atlasbiomed.com/blog/whats-going-on-with-hormones-and-neurotransmitters-during-sex/#:~:text=That%20we%20feel%20pleasure%20before,we%20really%20do%20feel%20enjoyment.

Dodgson, L. (2018). *Sex could improve your memory when you're older, according to a new study — further proof that it's good for the brain.* Accessed online: https://www.businessinsider.com/sex-could-improve-memory-2018-6?IR=T#:~:text=A%20new%20study%20has%20found,the%20brain%20associated%20with%20memory.

Editors of Encyclopaedia Britannica (n.d.). *Newton's laws of motion.* Accessed online (paraphrased): https://www.britannica.com/science/Newtons-laws-of-motion

Enejoh, V. et al (2015). *Impact of Self Esteem on Risky Behaviors among Nigerian Adolescents.* Accessed online: https://www.ncbi.nlm.nih.gov/pmc/articles/PMC4972583/

Foucault, (1976). *The History of Sexuality (Volume 1).*

Getting Horny: Understanding Your Sexual Response Cycle To Get Aroused (+11 Techniques). Accessed online: https://theprincessfantasy.com/blogs/news/getting-horny-understanding-your-sexual-response-cycle-to-get-aroused-11-techniques-1

Giuliano, F. (2011). *Neurophysiology of erection and ejaculation.* Accessed online: https://pubmed.ncbi.nlm.nih.gov/21967393/

Gruber & Grube (2000). *Adolescent sexuality and the media: a review of current knowledge and implications.* Accessed online: https://www.ncbi.nlm.nih.gov/pmc/articles/PMC1070813/

Gynecol, W.J.O. (2018). *Endorphins, oxytocin, sexuality and romantic relationships: An understudied area.* Accessed online: https://www.wjgnet.com/2218-6220/full/v7/i2/17.htm

Hession, R., (n.d.). *Brokenness – The Beginning of Revival.* Accessed online: https://heraldofhiscoming.org/index.php/read-the-herald/past-issues/162-past-issues/2009/mar09/2310-brokenness-the-beginning-of-revival-3-09

Horvath et al (n.d.). *Addictions: Sexual Addiction and Pornography Addiction.* Accessed online: https://www.gulfbend.org/poc/view_doc.php?type=doc&id=48517&cn=1408

Kansema, J., (2020). *How To Break Ungodly Soul Ties.* Accessed online: https://www.queenlyme.com/post/4-types-of-soul-ties-part-2#:~:text=Godly%20physical%20soul%20ties%20are,pat%20on%20the%20arm%2C%20ect.

Krans, B. (2019). *Want to Sleep Better? Have More Sex.* Accessed online: https://www.healthline.com/health-news/having-sex-more-often-can-help-you-sleep-better

Leuner, B., Glasper, E.R., & Gould, E. (2010). *Sexual Experience Promotes Adult Neurogenesis in the Hippocampus Despite an Initial Elevation in Stress Hormones.* Accessed online: https://journals.plos.org/plosone/article?id=10.1371/journal.pone.0011597

Lewis, C.S. (1942), *The Screwtape Letters.*

Maxwell, J.C. (2012) *The 15 Invaluable Laws of Growth.*

Nagoski online (2016): https://www.ted.com/talks/emily_nagoski_the_keys_to_a_happier_healthier_sex_life?language=en

Shpancer, N. (2012). *Why Do We Have Sex?* Accessed online: https://www.psychologytoday.com/za/blog/insight-therapy/201204/why-do-we-have-sex

Tolle, E. (2005). *A New Earth* (Page 9)

Van de Velde (n.d.). Accessed: file:///C:/Users/moonj/Dropbox/book/Van%20De%20Velde,%20Ideal%20Marriage%20.pdf

Vann, M.R. (2011). *Is Sex an Antidepressant?* Accessed online: https://www.everydayhealth.com/depression/is-sex-an-antidepressant.aspx#:~:text=One%20surprising%20recent%20study%20actually,and%20chemical%20compounds%20for%20women.

Vera Brinks*, Maaike van der Mark, Ronald de Kloet and Melly Oitzl: Division of Medical Pharmacology, LACDR⁄LUMC, Leiden University, The Netherlands

Wikipedia online: https://en.wikipedia.org/wiki/Fornication